BREAKING FREE

BREAKING FREE

A Recovery Workbook for Facing Codependence

Pia Mellody

and Andrea Wells Miller

HarperSanFrancisco

A Division of HarperCollins*Publishers*

LIBRARY OF CONGRESS CATALOGING-IN-PUBLICATION DATA

Mellody, Pia.
    Breaking free : a recovery workbook for facing codependence / Pia Mellody and Andrea Wells Miller. — 1st ed.
        p.   cm.
    ISBN 0-06-250590-4
    1. Codependents—Rehabilitation. 2. Self-care, Health.
I. Miller, Andrea Wells. II. Title.
RC569.5.C63M44   1989   88-45979
616.86--dc20   CIP

    90 91 92 93 MAL 10 9 8 7 6

Contents

Introduction

In *Facing Codependence* I define *codependence* as the lack of those functional internal habit patterns regarding the body, thinking, feeling, and behavior that are necessary to be a mature adult capable of having healthy relationships and finding a reasonable level of comfort in life.

This workbook is for people who want a self-help tool to assist in their recovery from codependence. It is a companion to *Facing Codependence: What It Is, Where It Comes From, How It Sabotages Our Lives*, which describes in detail the structure of the disease and where I believe it comes from.

I wrote this workbook to help people work through the initial sense of overwhelming devastation that often comes as they first become aware of the disease of codependence. I believe that at least four factors cause these overwhelming feelings:

1. The sheer number of symptoms identified as stemming from this disease.

2. The beginning awareness of how the disease got set up as you adapted to childhood experiences that were less than nurturing. This new awareness is especially crushing when the defenses used to protect yourself from the reality of what happened to you start to fail, and reality hits home.

3. The realization of the scope of the problem—how extensively the issues are affecting your life.

4. The seemingly slow progress you make in recovery, largely because much of the progress you do make is hidden by denial or minimized.

This fourth factor is curious and very important. Conducting life in the disease feels normal to a codependent. As you work at recovery, it is easier to be in the disease than to be functional. Being functional (acting in your own best interest) feels awful, shameful, as if you are doing something wrong. But in recovery you begin to see that what you thought was normal is actually dysfunctional, and you begin to *notice* yourself thinking, feeling, and acting in dysfunctional ways a lot. You learned to operate in this "normal" but dysfunctional way in childhood. You have been acting this way a long time and will find yourself continuing because it has been your standard operating procedure all along. This awareness is part of the process of recovery, and this book was designed to help you start to recover and to work against the experience of being overwhelmed and in denial, delusion, or minimization regarding your own recovery.

In my recovery, I found two avenues for help. One was therapy to (1) work on repressed and dissociated memories of childhood trauma, (2) work through shame core issues, and (3) be confronted regarding my disordered thinking and behavior. The second avenue involved using self-help tools that complemented what I was doing in therapy.

This workbook is designed to enhance self-help activities, although therapists can also use it to enhance work with a client whom they are treating for codependence. I believe that if you can write down (1) the scope of the problem (childhood trauma), (2) how you adapted so you came to see the disease as "normal," (3) how the disease works in your life today, and (4) most important, how you are actively changing, the balance will change so that you will begin to see more of your recovery rather than only the enormity of the disease.

This was true for me, and every exercise I suggest here I have done. This workbook is my gift to you born out of my life experience.

USING THIS WORKBOOK

This workbook goes hand in hand with *Facing Codependence*. We have made no attempt to reproduce all the information covered in *Facing Codependence*, but instead provide chapter and page references from *Facing Codependence* for background reading before you begin each exercise.

This workbook is organized around the three phases of recovery. Part 1 is designed to help you look at what happened in childhood and how you responded as a child, adapted to your dysfunctional family system, and developed the roots of your illness. Part 2 is structured to help you see how you are acting out your disease today, using the Twelve-Step process as a guide. Part 3 is set up to assist your recovery with exercises you can work through to confront your core symptoms, and use as a means of tracking your progress.

PART 1: BEYOND DENIAL ABOUT YOUR HISTORY OF ABUSE

Many codependents do not know that some of the things they experienced in their family of origin that seemed normal were, in fact, abusive and led to codependence. Seeing the total picture of your abusive childhood experience helps you move from minimization and denial into embracing reality. Providing that picture is the purpose of this part of the workbook.

Please note that recording your history here is not an occasion for attempting to reexperience profound or repressed feelings. It is merely a place to write down the information. If such feelings come up, it is a part of recovery to be able to connect them to specific incidents. However, *overwhelming feelings* are best handled with the help of a therapist.

PART 2: BEYOND THE DENIAL ABOUT YOUR CODEPENDENCE

Part 2 is a guideline I've developed for applying the Twelve Steps specifically to codependence. If you've seen some other guideline and want to use it, that's fine. But I believe it is important for each of us to write about the disease and how it looks in our own lives.

In the groups I lead and with the codependents I know, I use this motto: "Hug your demons or they'll bite you in the ass." To move into recovery you must begin identifying these adult codependency issues and do something about them or they will continue to interfere with your life through your relationships with others and, most important, with yourself. If you expect anybody else to address them for you, you will probably stay stuck, lost, and sick. Nobody else is supposed to do this work for you, and no one else can.

While it is true that your parents were responsible for helping you become a functional adult by exposing you to reality and treating you functionally and respectfully, it is necessary in recovery *not* to blame them for the condition of your life today. You must take charge of your own symptoms and recovery, by confronting your core symptoms, establishing functional habits, and thereby becoming an adult. This process is an act of taking charge of your life, or empowering yourself. Although acting in your own best interest may feel terrible at first, later as you get used to the experience of empowering and valuing yourself, it will feel very good.

PART 3: BEYOND DENIAL ABOUT YOUR RECOVERY

The third part of this workbook is designed to help you confront within yourself each core symptom of codependence: inappropriate levels of self-esteem, impaired boundaries, difficulty owning your reality, difficulty meeting your own needs and wants, and difficulty moderating your reality, expressing it at the appropriate age level. By confronting the symptoms, I mean beginning to take steps to recover from them, such as becoming aware of each symptom, then becoming able to intervene when they are operating, and doing exercises to strengthen your ability to intervene. I also include ways to write about your recovery from five different unmanageable consequences of the core symptoms. I have found that most people have a hard time staying aware of what the problems are unless they do a written Step One. In my experience, writing out Step One as outlined in part 2 before using any of the other means of confronting the symptoms of codependence is the most effective approach to recovery. The information you collect about your disease by writing out Step

One provides a necessary foundation for recovery, and writing it down helps you stay aware of the difficulties you experience because of codependence.

How Long Should You Spend Working on This Process?

This workbook is not intended to be something you can complete in an evening or even in two weeks. This process may take up to six months or more, because the information comes to our awareness gradually. It may be that you do some writing one day, then several weeks later receive a new piece of information as you begin to see more about how the illness is operating.

Recovery is a process, not an event. I believe that by moving through these pages at your own pace, writing all you can about each issue, and beginning to put into practice in your own life the suggestions given here, you will begin to find help in recovering from codependence.

Pia Mellody

Breaking Free from Denial:
Helpful Hints as You Begin

As you begin this workbook, you will find it very helpful to become aware of ways your mind and body can either hinder or help your search for information about your codependence and healing from it. Following are some hints about recognizing defense mechanisms that can obstruct your progress, and ways your body can release information to you that can lead to clearer memories about your childhood. This section also suggests ground rules for doing the exercises. Find a quiet place to read for thirty minutes and complete the reading assignments in this section before beginning Part 1.

RECOGNIZING DEFENSE MECHANISMS

BACKGROUND READING

Chapter 9 of *Facing Codependence*. (Please read this chapter before continuing.)

Codependence has some built-in obstacles that can get in the way of your being able to make any real and lasting changes. They are the same protective devices you developed in childhood to color the reality of what was happening to you to make it more pleasant or put the painful reality out of mind so you could survive. I think you can move through the obstacles more easily if you are at least aware of them and ready to accept that they are operating in you.

In *Facing Codependence*, I deal with six defense mechanisms, divided into two groups. The first group consists of suppression, repression, and the more profound defense of dissociation. The second group includes minimization, denial, and the more profound defense of delusion. Descriptions and examples of each one are in the assigned background reading.

Part 1 of this workbook is a guideline for reviewing your childhood experiences to see how they created your codependence. The more you can become consciously aware of what happened to you in childhood, the easier your recovery will be. So it's very important to go back over your past memories and begin to *work through the various defense mechanisms you have developed so you can recapture important events you have lost.* (This process of dealing with your defense mechanisms and what they are trying to conceal continues for the rest of your life, by the way.)

DEFENSES ARE RESPONSIBLE FOR CONFUSING AND/OR DISTRESSING BEHAVIOR

Because of this network of defenses that hides or camouflages any behavior or memory that might be threatening to the reputation of your family system, you might find that as an adult you exhibit behavior that is confusing or distressing to you. Or you may find yourself married to a person who is dysfunctional and abusive, yet you stay in the relationship anyway. And since you have little or no clear memory of what happened in your family of origin, it's hard to see that you may have married someone who can help you reproduce all or parts of the familiar abusive system in which you were raised. Instead, you may believe you're crazy, which is the primary complaint that codependents offer when they first come for help. "I feel nuts. Something's not connected."

Part of feeling crazy is due to not being conscious of your history, which is extremely important to you and which can be the doorway to freedom from its control. Being aware that these defense mechanisms are obstacles to freedom, and that they continue to operate in you as part of codependence, can help you begin to recognize specific occurrences of them in your own adult life and become aware of how they may be blocking you from seeing not only your history but also your current symptoms and their unmanageable consequences.

So it is a critical part of recovery for you to know the following:

· What the defense mechanisms are

· How they work in your life

Your recovery will also be helped by accepting these facts:

· These defenses still operate in adult codependents.

· Your own defenses are usually invisible to you.

· For recovery, you must allow other trusted people to confront those defenses by telling you when they think you are using them.

· Although it will be hard and you may feel fear or anger at the time, you must listen to these confrontations in order to break through the defenses to recovery.

Here is a brief review of the defenses you read about in *Facing Codependence*, chapter 9.

SUPPRESSION, REPRESSION, AND DISSOCIATION

The first three defenses are suppression, repression, and dissociation. When these are still operating in you in adulthood, they remove much of your history from your conscious mind.

Suppression is consciously choosing to forget things that are too painful to remember. You make a decision to put the memory away, or to "forget," so that you don't have to feel the painful or unacceptable feelings associated with it.

Repression is automatically and unconsciously forgetting things that are too painful to remember. Such painful and frightening memories are "automatically" shifted into the unconscious mind where they are "lost" or hidden.

A child using *dissociation* psychologically takes his or her emotional and mental self away somewhere where the abuse is not experienced in full. In other words, the child no longer experiences the abuse at the intense emotional and mental level at which the physical pain is felt, although the physical body of the child is still being abused.

Children usually reserve dissociation to survive abuse they believe is life-threatening, such as incest, molestation, or being beaten until they think the beating is going to kill them. The fear is either that who they are is going to be destroyed, or that they'll be physically destroyed.

MINIMIZATION, DENIAL, AND DELUSION

Minimization, denial, and delusion are the other three defense mechanisms we are discussing. When these operate in you as an adult, they allow you to have your history, but cause you to skew it or distort it so that you can't see it accurately.

These are most often used in the adult stage of life. An adult doing abusive things to his or her children uses minimization, denial, and delusion to avoid facing the reality that his or her actions are abusive. And the "adult child" who must emotionally deal with the memories of his or her childhood uses these three defenses to avoid the painful reality that his or her beloved parent was abusive and his or her childhood was not "wonderful."

Minimization means you see what happened to you as less serious or important than it would be had the same thing happened to someone else.

Denial is in operation when you can see and grasp certain realities in other people's lives, but can't see that the same realities apply in your own life. You have intellectual awareness of the abusive event, but can't feel any feelings about it. You might agree that something was abusive for another person, but say, "In my case that happened, but it wasn't abusive to me."

Delusion is a process that is more profound and serious. Delusion means you believe something in spite of the facts, which means you hear the facts but don't assign the proper meaning to them. A person in delusion can hear or read that a certain situation is abusive for a child and just disregard the information, believing that the situation isn't abusive for anyone.

A serious problem with delusion is that like all the other defenses, it's invisible to you and you don't know you are deluded. This is a very dangerous and vulnerable position to be in, since reality itself and anyone with a strong sense of reality tend to threaten the view you have of your world. So people in delusion tend to isolate themselves from those who might reveal the truth about their lives.

Often the resistance to acknowledging something as abusive stems from the fact that the person is *repeating* the same abuse to his or her own children and doesn't want to recognize it as abusive. People in this situation can't see that they are resisting. They just stick to the "facts" of their own deluded view.

GROUND RULES FOR GATHERING INFORMATION

BACKGROUND READING

Chapter 8 of *Facing Codependence.*

To begin the recovery process, you must recapture memories of abusive incidents in your childhood. The following is a condensed review of the guidelines you read in *Facing Codependence* that will help keep you focused on this information-gathering task and make it easier.

1. Look only at your life from birth to age seventeen.

2. Identify the major caregivers who did the abusive things to you. Major caregivers are the people who were in a position of power or control over you and had access to you to abuse you (for example, parents, grandparents, aunts, uncles, older cousins, older siblings, doctors, counselors, priests, nuns, ministers, scout leaders, teachers, babysitters, even strangers who may have frightened you).

3. Avoid focusing on whether the person who did the abuse *meant* to harm you or not. When you're at the point of getting your history straight, it is actually irrelevant whether somebody meant to abuse you or not, and my experience has been that the majority of major caregivers who abuse children do not mean to.

4. Do not blame the major caregiver for your codependence. The purpose of looking at who abused you is to be able to hold them accountable in your mind and separate the act of abuse done to you from any sense you may have of being inferior or responsible for it.

   Blame means you believe you have the problems you have because of what somebody else did to you. This gives power to the offender and renders you, the victim, powerless—without the ability to protect yourself or change. Therefore, blaming will keep you stuck in the disease and will probably make you worse.

   Accountability means you acknowledge that the abuse happened and who did it, but you can do what you need to do to protect yourself and make the changes necessary to recover from the abuse of your past. This attitude gives you the power to move into recovery and develop tools with which to deal with life, whether the offender ever changes or not.

5. Do not compare your history to someone else's. Such comparison can quickly lead to minimization and denial. *Whatever happened to you was important.* If it seemed as though it was abusive to you, it was abusive.

6. Strike these four words from your vocabulary as you describe your history: *good*, *bad*, *right*, and *wrong*. They're very judgmental words and using them makes it hard to hold anybody you care for accountable for what they did.

   Instead, when describing behavior that was very painful and less than nurturing, use the word *dysfunctional*. And when you talk about behavior that was nurturing, that helped you feel good about yourself, use the word *functional*. In addition to the term *dysfunctional*, I also use the terms *abusive* and *less than nurturing* throughout this workbook to mean the same thing.

7. Keep your focus on your caregivers, NOT on *yourself as a caregiver*. Focusing on your behavior toward your own children at this point can interfere with your recovery because you're so busy focusing on how "horrible" you are that you don't have to look at your own abuse issues from your history.

AIDS TO RECOVERING MEMORIES

I have found two helpful indicators that, if followed, often lead to recovery of buried memories: body memories and feeling memories. These are like security passwords to a carefully guarded computer program. Once the computer operator enters the password into the computer, the program can be accessed. In a similar way, once you recognize a feeling or body memory, you may be able to follow that memory and gain access to data in the unconscious mind about abuse you suppressed, repressed, or dissociated from when it originally happened. The body can allow you to return a lost memory to the conscious mind via a physical or emotional sensation that can't be explained by anything that's actually happening to you at that moment. This valuable data can then be brought to your conscious mind (with the help of a skillful therapist) so that you can work through the feelings around the memory and begin to heal from it.

A *body memory* is a sudden unusual physical symptom that doesn't appear to be related to any physical cause at the moment. For example, you may be sitting comfortably, reading this book, but all of a sudden get a piercing pain in your head, or feel dizzy, or feel a wave of nausea. Perhaps your arm suddenly aches as if it had been kicked, or your throat hurts as if someone were choking you. Suddenly, you may sense a hand on the back of your neck pinching you or feel a pain in the area of your groin. Such sensations are body memories.

A *feeling memory* is a sudden overwhelming emotional experience that also cannot be explained by anything that you are aware of at the moment.

Feeling memories surface in the form of four primary emotions: anger, fear, pain, and shame. I also call feeling memories "feeling attacks," since they seem to come suddenly and uninvited out of nowhere. When a feeling attack comes in the form of anger, it is a "rage attack." When it's in the form of fear, it's a "panic attack" or a "paranoia attack." A feeling memory of pain is a sudden overwhelming sense of hopelessness, often followed by a thought of suicide. And a feeling memory of shame (called a "shame attack") is a sudden, profound, almost overwhelming sense of being less-than, worthless, inadequate, bad, stupid, or ugly (such words about yourself often come to you in the process of a shame attack). A feeling memory is almost always experienced as an overwhelming feeling.

These two current manifestations of buried memory (body and feeling memories) indicate to me that our minds are so powerful that although we can bury memories in our unconscious mind and "know but not know," our bodies *never* forget and will keep trying to let us see the truth about ourselves.

Many times these feeling and body memories can be used as doorways to take you back into remembering what really did happen in your childhood and retrieving long-repressed events in your personal history.

SPONTANEOUS REGRESSION

As you learned in the background reading, spontaneous regression takes place almost always in a therapeutic situation that is guided by the counselor. I described it so that you will know what it is, but since you are merely writing about your history in this book, your emotional experience will be less intense than that experienced in therapy, and thus will probably not be intense enough to trigger such a regression.

If you should find yourself experiencing a regression, however, contact in person or on the telephone someone who will understand this phenomenon. Tell the person that you were reading about abuse or writing about your history when all of a sudden you started having these intense feelings; then describe the feelings. This will usually bring you back in touch with the present. If the feelings persist, call someone with therapeutic training and ask that person for help.

RECOVERY BEGINS
WITH PUTTING YOUR HISTORY TOGETHER

Reviewing your life from birth to age seventeen with regard to what happened between you and your major caregivers (without blaming or worrying about whether these caregivers intended to hurt you) is a way to begin to put your history together. Other subtle but powerful ways of getting in touch with these important memories include listening to people in a therapy group tell about their histories or tell you what defenses they see you using; following body and feeling memories; and (in therapy) experiencing regressions. Memories that have been consigned to the unconscious mind by suppression, repression, and dissociation, or distorted by minimization, denial, and delusion can be retrieved as the first steps toward healing the precious child within who experienced them.

In the first part of this workbook, you begin to focus on specific less-than-nurturing experiences in your childhood. You begin to see how the illness of codependence operated in your family of origin and how within that family you adapted into a codependent.

BREAKING FREE

Part 1

Beyond Denial About Your History of Abuse

Your History of Abuse

The experience of abuse in childhood is the root of the illness of codependence. I believe the recovery process begins by looking at the beginning of the disease—which is in childhood. A dysfunctional, less-than-nurturing, abusive system could not help you mature. Instead, that environment caused you to adapt so that your parents could be comfortable. You adapted yourself into the habits that make up codependence.

I believe that examining the specific events that make up your history as a codependent serves three important purposes:

1. Writing about your history shows you how your parents' attitude toward and treatment of you affected each specific characteristic you had as a child: your sense of value, your vulnerability, your imperfection, your dependency, and your sense of how to act your age. As you bring up these incidents and remember them, you can begin to see exactly the moment when the abuse was creating your disease.

2. Writing about specific events enables you to connect your feelings to your history. When you were a child, you felt pain, fear, anger, or shame about what was being done to you that was abusive, even though you did not know it was abusive. Children in an abusive family system rarely get to talk about the feelings they're having, because often if they express their feelings, their parents go out of control and react abusively to them. So they have to hold the feelings in, and the feelings collect and increase in intensity throughout the childhood years.

   Some children go through childhood constantly overloaded with intense emotions. Other children defend themselves from overwhelming emotions by freezing their feeling reality. By this I mean they deaden their conscious awareness of the feelings in the body.

   However, strong emotions do not go away but remain within you looking for some form of expression. As I've often heard in recovery groups, you can either act them out, stuff them, or deal with them appropriately. As a codependent you experience unhealthy expressions of these old feelings in the form of surprising explosive feeling attacks such as rage, panic, debilitating shame, or depression. You may also experience unnecessary illnesses due to the stress of keeping the feelings locked away inside you.

To recover, you must release from your body the childhood feelings you had about being abused. To deal with all these powerful old feelings, you must bring the feelings to your consciousness, feel them in your body, acknowledge the feelings mentally by connecting them to what happened to you, verbalize them, and let yourself stay in the feelings while someone supports you by listening. You must allow the child you were to talk through the adult part of yourself about what happened and how you felt about it.

The only way you can connect the feelings to what happened is to know what happened. The purpose of writing your history down is to reconnect those lost feelings with what happened.

All that is necessary for this process is to describe what happened in as much detail as you can remember, and then connect the feelings to the memory by naming the emotions you felt then and feel now. "This is what happened to me and I am angry and hurt about that now" (or whatever your feelings were at the time and are now).

If you just say generally, "My childhood was awful. I have a lot of pain about that and I'm not going to talk about it again because I don't want to get back into it," you can't go through this healing process of resolving the feelings connected directly to specific memories.

Many people fear that opening themselves up to these feelings will either overwhelm them or leave them in a permanent state of feeling intense anger, pain, fear, and shame. But this isn't true. I've worked with people who go through this process repeatedly. Each time they do, I see that their feelings are a little less intense, until they can tell the story of what happened without having intense feelings. Reexperiencing those feelings (or perhaps experiencing them for the first time) for the purpose of resolving them by this process will bring relief. It is by this process of letting yourself experience these childhood feelings that you release them.

3. Writing about your childhood experiences enables you to look at how you recreate the same emotional atmosphere today. A well-documented characteristic of people who were raised in dysfunctional families is that they often choose to relate to people who create the same emotional atmosphere they knew in their family of origin. They recreate many of the dynamics of their childhood dysfunctional family system in their lives today. Recovery becomes much more difficult because as the things that happened in childhood are recreated in their adult lives, they start reacting to the people they are living with now the way they reacted back then.

You must identify how your family of origin operated so you can change the way you handle relationships in your life today. If you don't go back and look at the dysfunctional dynamics of your family of origin, it is virtually impossible to look at the dysfunctional conduct going on in your family today.

My guess is that most of us recreate childhood dynamics in our adult relationships in an effort to resolve those old painful and often denied feelings. The problem is that the feelings cannot be resolved in this way. Instead, the intensity of our feelings increases.

Eventually, if you're in touch with your feelings, you sense you're in the same old problems, so you leave the relationship, thinking you just need a different relationship to avoid this problem. Instead of resolving feelings, you wind up blaming other people in your life for what's going on with you. You've recreated the same family dynamics and have surrounded yourself with people who produce the same emotional atmosphere, so you do not have healthy, functional relationships.

Keep in mind as you begin to go through your memories of childhood that it is vital to begin to identify the feelings you had as a child and also the ones you still have today when you remember those incidents. Do not skip this section.

However, it is important to note that this is only a *beginning point* for recovery. As you work through this section you may feel worse for a while because of all the emotions you are identifying and feeling. When you move on to part 2 and look at what is going on in your adult life and how to intervene in that, you will start to feel better emotionally. Resist the temptation to stay stuck in these feelings related to childhood experiences.

This section of the workbook provides space to write down your memories of abusive incidents, so that in later sections you can connect the memories to your feelings and then go through the process of resolution. *It is not intended for you to go into the process of resolving the feelings now.* However, while writing these memories, you may tap into some old feelings, but that is part of the process of recovery. Even though the feelings are intense, they must be connected to the specific events for you to get beyond the feelings.

If you should tap into some feelings, continue to write while feeling them. Your face may feel flushed and hot from shame, you may have tears running down your face from pain, or you may feel your heart beating from fear or anger, but as long as these feelings are reasonable in intensity and do not impair your thinking process, continue writing. If the feelings are too powerful or overwhelming for you to think clearly or write well, stop writing and contact someone safe such as your sponsor, a nonjudgmental friend, or your therapist if you have one. Tell that person what you were doing, the incident you were thinking about, and what feelings you are having. If the feelings remain unresolved and you stay upset or they come and go as days go by, I recommend that you talk to a professional counselor about the situation.

BACKGROUND READING

In *Facing Codependence*, I have divided abuse into five categories. Each category should be examined as you go through your childhood memories to write about your less-than-nurturing experiences. Before you begin to write about each category, read the corresponding chapter in *Facing Codependence*.

Physical abuse:	chapter 10
Sexual abuse:	chapter 11
Emotional abuse:	chapter 12
Intellectual abuse:	chapter 13
Spiritual abuse:	chapter 14

WHAT TO DO

In the blank chart that follows, list examples of abuse you experienced during childhood (age: birth to seventeen). For one caregiver at a time, write about every instance of abuse you can remember with that caregiver in each of the five areas of abuse. Do this in the following manner:

1. Name one caregiver.

2. Take one kind of abuse and list all the incidents you remember involving the caregiver. List them in chronological order from your youngest age to your oldest.

3. Describe briefly what happened in each case.

4. List one or more emotions you felt about each incident at the time, and how you feel now as you remember it. (To keep this exercise simple, select from these four feelings: shame, anger, fear, pain. For example, sadness and loneliness would be forms of pain, anxiety a form of fear, and rage a form of anger.)

5. After you complete the first abuse category, list the next one and all the incidents in that category involving the same caregiver. Again, list them in chronological order.

6. Continue working with your memory of that caregiver until you have worked through each kind of abuse.

7. Then list the next caregiver and start over with the first category of abuse.

EXAMPLE

TYPE OF ABUSE	WHO DID IT	YOUR AGE	WHAT HAPPENED	HOW YOU FELT	
				THEN	NOW
Physical	Mom	4	Slapped my face when I called my 2-year-old sister a dummy.	pain shame	anger pain shame
Intellectual	"	4–12	Told me I was stupid.	fear pain shame	shame anger pain
Emotional	"	10	Told me not to cry when my dog died.	fear	shame fear anger
Sexual	"	14–17	Made me talk to her after dates. Made me tell her details about my sexual conduct.	shame anger	shame anger
Spiritual	"	5	Accused me of stealing money from her, then found the money but did not tell me or apologize. My big brother told me she found it. She could not admit mistakes to me.	shame fear anger pain	shame fear RAGE pain

My History of Childhood Abuse

TYPE OF ABUSE	WHO DID IT	YOUR AGE	WHAT HAPPENED	HOW YOU FELT	
				THEN	NOW

My History of Childhood Abuse

TYPE OF ABUSE	WHO DID IT	YOUR AGE	WHAT HAPPENED	HOW YOU FELT	
				THEN	NOW

My History of Childhood Abuse

TYPE OF ABUSE	WHO DID IT	YOUR AGE	WHAT HAPPENED	HOW YOU FELT THEN	NOW

My History of Childhood Abuse

TYPE OF ABUSE	WHO DID IT	YOUR AGE	WHAT HAPPENED	HOW YOU FELT THEN	NOW

My History of Childhood Abuse

TYPE OF ABUSE	WHO DID IT	YOUR AGE	WHAT HAPPENED	HOW YOU FELT	
				THEN	NOW

How That Abuse Affected You

PURPOSE OF EXERCISE

When beginning to construct a picture of your childhood history, it is helpful to review not only how your family was less than nurturing, but also how dysfunctional parenting led to your codependence. This section provides space to look at how your experience of abuse began to set up your disease of codependence.

BACKGROUND READING

Chapters 5 and 6 of *Facing Codependence.*

Every child has certain universal traits when he or she is born. The child cannot choose to be otherwise. These characteristics are the foundation for becoming a mature, functional adult. If the child's parents do not understand and encourage (accept and direct rather than reject and coerce to change) these as *natural, normal* characteristics then the parents are very likely to abuse their child through dysfunctional parenting techniques. Thus, a child can suffer profound damage through the stunting or negating of these crucial given characteristics.

These five characteristics of the child and their fully developed expression in a mature adult are outlined in the charts on the following page.

A Child Is Naturally . . .	A Mature, Functional Adult Is . . .
VALUABLE	Self-esteeming from inside
VULNERABLE	Vulnerable, with protection
IMPERFECT	Able to embrace self as perfectly imperfect and be accountable for imperfection that damages others. Able to look to a Higher Power for help with imperfections.
DEPENDENT (NEEDING, WANTING)	Interdependent
IMMATURE	Mature at own age level

The core symptoms of codependence that develop out of experiencing less-than-nurturing parenting during childhood are as follows:

A Child Is Naturally . . .	A Codependent Adult Has . . .
VALUABLE	Difficulty experiencing appropriate levels of self-esteem
VULNERABLE	Difficulty setting functional boundaries
IMPERFECT	Difficulty owning and expressing own reality
DEPENDENT (NEEDING, WANTING)	Difficulty taking care of own needs and wants
IMMATURE	Difficulty experiencing and expressing reality moderately and at appropriate age level

WHAT TO DO

Write about how each incident of abuse you listed in the previous exercise affected each of the five natural characteristics you had as a child: (1) your sense of your own value, (2) your vulnerability, (3) your imperfection, (4) your needs and wants and your ability to get help to meet them, and (5) your sense of acting your own age. Do this in the following manner:

1. From the previous exercises, copy your first incident in the second column of the following blank chart. Enter your age in the first column.

2. Write each of the five characteristics in the third column.

3. In the fourth column, write in your own words the message that you received about each characteristic from the incident with your caregiver.

4. Copy your second incident from the previous exercise, followed by each of the five characteristics. Then put the message you received in the fourth column.

You may find that you cannot perceive a message for each of the five characteristics. Feel free to leave blank spaces beside characteristics for which no message seems apparent at this time. Any message you may have gotten will perhaps become clear to you later on.

You may find the same message recurring for a given characteristic as you work through this exercise, or you may find that the messages were different with different experiences.

EXAMPLE	AGE	EVENT	CHARACTERISTIC	MESSAGE
	4	Mom slapped my face when I called my 2-year-old sister a dummy.	value	I am not valuable when I express my thoughts.
			vulnerability	My mother has the right to hurt my body.
			imperfection	There are painful consequences when I am imperfect.
			dependency	I will be attacked when I need correcting.
			immaturity	I should act the way an older child would act.

How Abuse Affected Me

AGE	EVENT	CHARACTERISTIC	MESSAGE

How Abuse Affected Me

AGE	EVENT	CHARACTERISTIC	MESSAGE

How Abuse Affected Me

AGE	EVENT	CHARACTERISTIC	MESSAGE

How Abuse Affected Me

AGE	EVENT	CHARACTERISTIC	MESSAGE

How Abuse Affected Me

AGE	EVENT	CHARACTERISTIC	MESSAGE

Before going on to the next section, check back through the specific examples of abuse in the previous exercise ("Your History of Abuse") and see if you can fill in any additional incidents and their effects on your basic characteristics. Then go on to part 2.

Part 2

BEYOND DENIAL
ABOUT YOUR
CODEPENDENCE

Introduction

Now that you have a clearer picture of what went on in your childhood that created your codependence, the next part of the solution begins with identifying how the distorted internal habit patterns are operating in your life in the present.

I see codependence as a disease of immaturity, rendering a person unable to experience appropriate levels of self-esteem, unable to set boundaries with other people, unable to own his or her own reality, unable to take care of his or her needs and wants appropriately, and unable to express his or her reality moderately and at the appropriate age level.

I see the five core symptoms as developmental problems of maturation in this way: all children have to learn certain things to eventually become adults emotionally and mentally by the time their physical bodies mature. They must learn to esteem themselves, to have boundaries, to own their own reality, to take care of their needs and wants, and to express themselves with moderation. When these functions are not developed or are developed dysfunctionally, emotional and mental maturity does not accompany physical maturity. Therefore, I often describe codependents as "little people in big bodies."

Those who suffer from codependence engage in dysfunctional (self-defeating) patterns of appearing, thinking, feeling, and/or behaving that prevent them from experiencing relationships and life fully as mature adults. As a result of codependence, we do not know how to relate functionally to ourselves. (Many codependents wonder "Who am I?" or are harsh, punitive, and neglectful toward themselves, or undisciplined and self-indulgent.) We also do not know how to relate functionally to others: a spouse, children, co-workers, friends.

As children we do not know whether or not our caregivers are functional, but we assume they are. So if they are dysfunctional, shaming, and insecure, and living with them seems pain-filled, lonely, empty, or otherwise difficult, we assume it is due to our own defects. Since contact with major caregivers teaches us how to relate to others, the illness of codependence begins to develop while we are living with them. *We come to believe that the emotional reactions and behaviors that are hallmarks of codependence are normal, and we continue to believe so as adults.* Thus, as adult codependents, we do not recognize the silent, deadly, programmed illness of codependence operating in our lives.

We codependents have adult-looking bodies but we lack the internal habit patterns necessary to think, feel, and behave as adults. We have not matured properly to be at our own age level, so we are "little people in great big bodies." *To recognize and arrest codependence, we must become able to both experience and identify it as a disease, not normalcy.*

Part 2 of this workbook is designed to help you confront codependence by using the Twelve-Step process* as a guide.

* The Twelve-Step process uses the Twelve Steps first developed by Alcoholics Anonymous. Codependents Anonymous supports people in recovery from codependence by means of meetings and the same Twelve Steps, which have been adapted for codependents. To find out about meetings in your city, check the white business pages of your telephone book for a local number. If there is no number, contact the national office by mail or telephone. The address is Codependents Anonymous, P.O. Box 33577, Phoenix, AZ 85067–3577. The telephone number is (602)944–0141.

OVERVIEW OF CODEPENDENCE

Natural Characteristics of a Child	Dysfunctional Survival Traits	Core or Primary Symptoms of Adult Codependence	Consequences of Core Symptoms	
			Secondary Symptoms†	Dysfunctional Parenting of Our Children
Valuable	Less-than or *Better-than	Difficulty experiencing appropriate levels of self-esteem	Negative control (controlling the reality of others for our own comfort)	Inability to appropriately esteem our children
Vulnerable	Too vulnerable or *Invulnerable	Difficulty setting functional boundaries	Resentment (having a need to punish others for wrongs we perceive they have done to us)	Inability to avoid abusing our children
Imperfect	Bad/rebellious or *Good/perfect	Difficulty owning and expressing our own reality and imperfection	Distorted or nonexistent spirituality (having difficulty experiencing connection to a power greater than self)	Inability to allow our children to have their reality and be imperfect
Dependent (needing, wanting)	Too dependent or *Antidependent or Needless/wantless	Difficulty taking care of our adult needs and wants	Avoiding reality (using addictions, physical illness, or mental illness to avoid our own reality)	Inability to appropriately nurture our children
Immature	Extremely immature (Chaotic) or *Overmature (Controlling)	Difficulty experiencing and expressing our reality moderately	Impaired intimacy (having difficulty sharing who we are with others and hearing them share who they are)	Inability to provide a stable environment for our children

* Our culture believes that the better-than, invulnerable, perfectionistic, antidependent, and controlling person is healthy. But in fact these are codependent characteristics and are much *more* difficult to treat than the characteristics at the other extreme: less-than, too vulnerable, rebellious, too dependent, and chaotic.

† The absence of horizontal lines in this column indicates that these elements are *not* related one-on-one with the other items across the same horizontal row, but result from any combination of the core symptoms and lead to any of the dysfunctional parenting components.

Step One

> *"We admitted we were powerless over ourselves and that our lives had become unmanageable."**

I have divided Step One into two sets of exercises around the two key words *powerless* and *unmanageable.* I believe it is necessary to write about both how you are powerless and how your life is unmanageable to fully make the admissions required by this step.

You will explore the specific way you experience powerlessness over your codependence by writing about each *core symptom.* You will explore the unmanageability you experience as a result of your codependence by writing about *what happens as a result of these symptoms.*

The writing you do for Step One will provide a base of information that you will be using throughout the rest of the steps. The more thorough you can be at this stage, the more benefit you will get from the later steps.

Powerlessness Over Codependence

PURPOSE OF EXERCISES

These exercises are designed to help you see more clearly how the five core symptoms of codependence are operating in your life. By getting very specific in your descriptions, you can begin to move beyond denial — out of the general awareness that "Yes, I am a codependent," into knowing precisely which thoughts, feelings, and behaviors are codependent and how they are affecting your life.

* The wording of this step from Codependents Anonymous is "We admitted we were powerless over *others,* and that our lives had become unmanageable." In my opinion, however, we ourselves affect our relationships with others, so I use the word *ourselves* in this step for the purposes of this workbook.

In addition to doing the background reading assigned in this workbook, going to Twelve-Step meetings such as Codependents Anonymous is a very helpful way to come out of denial and delusion and stop minimizing. Listening to people describe their experiences with these symptoms can often trigger a realization of your own experience with a symptom. If you have an opportunity to chair a meeting, suggest that the topic of discussion be the symptom you are writing about. Share what you have learned about yourself so far, then listen to the discussion. Even if you are not chairing, you can share your own discoveries, which often prompts others to share theirs about the same problem. Of course, meetings are beneficial for both working through the rest of the steps and after you've been completely through the steps the first time. But they can be especially helpful during your writing of Step One.

In *Facing Codependence*, I have identified five core or primary symptoms of codependence that arise when a child in a dysfunctional family is not helped to develop or mature. These core symptoms seem to describe what child abuse actually does to a person. I look at each one as an *issue of powerlessness* because when you are experiencing any specific symptom you can't stop it from happening. You are operating from an automatic, deeply grooved pattern, and thus rendered powerless to act like a mature adult (for example, feeling great shame when you make a simple mistake in front of someone). Also, the symptoms take over without your knowing they are happening to you.

In my opinion, the first core symptom, difficulty experiencing appropriate levels of self-esteem, is the most crucial. The second most important is difficulty setting functional boundaries. I have found that these two core symptoms must be treated before the other three symptoms can be adequately addressed, so I strongly suggest taking these symptoms in the order presented in this workbook.

Complete the suggested background reading before you write about each symptom. Read about one symptom at a time, then do the writing about that symptom before reading about the next symptom.

As a reminder, this exercise is not meant to be completed in an evening or even a week of daily writing. Don't worry if you need to spend a month or longer on it. As your denial, minimization, and delusion gradually recede you will be able to write a little more.

CORE SYMPTOM 1:
DIFFICULTY EXPERIENCING APPROPRIATE LEVELS OF SELF-ESTEEM

BACKGROUND READING

Pages 7–10 in chapter 2 of *Facing Codependence*. Here is a brief summary of the background reading:

Healthy self-esteem is the internal experience of your own value, or preciousness. It is generated within yourself, rather than coming to you from outside through the positive regard of other people, accomplishments, or possessions. When you experience healthy self-esteem, you know that no matter what mistakes you make or how you look or what your grades were at school or what other people say, you are worthwhile, lovable, and adequate.

When you cannot experience healthy self-esteem, you experience esteem in one of two inappropriate ways. At one end of the spectrum is the experience of low or no self-esteem. At the other end is the experience of arrogance and grandiosity, of being better than others. And when you cannot esteem yourself from within, you get your vital supply of esteem from outside, which is what I call "other-esteem."

Codependents operate from arrogance and grandiosity in two different ways. One way is by using arrogance and grandiosity to cover the pain of feeling less than others. The other is actually believing you are better than others and not experiencing any feelings of being less than others. Either situation is dysfunctional.

Everybody has equal value. You may have different assets (or talents or abilities) that are more than or less than others', but all of us are equally precious, full of worth, and valuable as people.

The state of powerlessness related to this core symptom is this: whenever you encounter another person, you perceive that person as having either less value or more value than you. When you are doing either one you are operating in the disease of codependence. Describing how you do either one brings your state of powerlessness over this symptom of codependence out of denial and into the open.

WHAT TO DO

In the column on the left, describe the situations that trigger your sense of being of less value than other people. Then, in the column on the right, describe your thinking about how you are of less value than others.

EXAMPLE

SITUATION	*MY THINKING AND FEELINGS*
When I see someone driving an expensive car	I think he's dong better financially than I am and is therefore more valuable.
When I go to a party and my dress is not what everyone else is wearing	The others are more valuable or important than I am. I also feel ugly.
When someone asks me a question I can't answer	I feel stupid and that the person who asked me is smarter than I am.
When I see another woman whose beauty I can see and recognize	I regard myself as ugly and therefore of less value.
When I realize someone has more education than I do	I think the person is smarter than I and I feel stupid and inadequate.

My Experience of Low Self-Esteem

SITUATION	MY THINKING AND FEELINGS

Describe how you fail to act in your own best interest when you are feeling of less value than others.

EXAMPLE

When I'm aware of my fatigue and thinking that I need to lie down and rest, but my wife says that right now we need to go do an errand she's been waiting for me to do with her, I start to think that her thinking is better than mine. I fail to value my own thinking and tell her how tired I am and then go rest. Instead I go ahead and do the errand, even though it isn't in my best interest.

I was invited to a horror movie, and I knew that it would not be entertaining to me and that afterward I would have to deal with nightmares and tension. But my friend laughed at me and said, "Oh come on. It's just a movie." At that moment I believed I'm worth less than my friend who is not "afraid" of the movie, and then went ahead and endured seeing the movie.

When I realized I couldn't afford to buy an expensive dress for the office Christmas party, I avoided going to the party and robbed myself of a potentially pleasant time.

When I think that another person has more valuables than I do, and I start feeling worthless, I gossip about that person, saying derogatory things about him or her, and later have to face the adverse effect on the other person and the bad feelings about myself.

How I Fail to Act in My Own Best Interest Due to Feeling I Am of Less Value Than Others

Describe how you view yourself as being of more value than others.

EXAMPLE	Cindy often writes hot checks and can't seem to keep her financial records straight. Her apartment is disorganized and she is almost always late. As I look at her life, I judge her to be inferior to me because my checkbook is balanced, my home is well kept, and I am usually on time.
	When another person shares her thinking with me and I see that it is different from mine, I automatically decide she is stupid and I am superior in my thinking and she is inferior.
	When I notice that my wife is in a lot of pain, I judge her to be "emotional" and out of control and therefore I feel superior and think that she is of less value.
	When I notice that my husband never shows any feelings and changes the subject when I try to talk about mine, I judge him to be "stuffing" his feelings and avoiding issues and I feel superior because I can feel my feelings.
	I feel better than a person who has less education than I do and speaks poor English.
	I feel better than a person who has a mental or physical handicap.
	I feel better than a person who does not think as fast as I can.
	I feel better than a person who is very unattractive.

How I Have Viewed Myself as Being of More Value Than Others

Describe how you become abusive to others when you feel you are of more value than they are.

EXAMPLE	When Cindy is late for something we are doing together, I use sarcastic jokes or earnest talks about her "problems" in an effort to help her. I give myself permission to tell her what to do in order for me to be comfortable.
	When I feel superior to my wife because she is being "emotional" and out of control, I am abusive by telling her she is just being "emotional" and ridiculing her. Or sometimes I offer to "help" her get control of herself, which is actually my attempting to control her feelings so I can be comfortable.
	When I feel superior to my husband because he avoids his feelings, I am abusive by raging and attacking him about the way he deals with feelings—or fails to deal with them. Sometimes I try to control his feeling reality, offering to "help" him get in touch with his feelings. But the real motivation is so I can be more comfortable.

How I Become Abusive to Others When I Feel More Valuable Than They Are

CORE SYMPTOM 2:
DIFFICULTY SETTING FUNCTIONAL BOUNDARIES

BACKGROUND READING

Pages 11–21 in chapter 2 of *Facing Codependence.* Here is a brief summary of the background reading:

Functional adults use intact, flexible boundaries to protect themselves externally and internally and to keep from transgressing the boundaries of and authentically offending others. (An "authentic offense" or "authentic act of abuse" is an act that disregards another person's boundaries. There may be instances when someone may not like or be happy about what he or she observes you thinking, feeling, and doing, and may say, "I'm offended by that." But that is NOT what I mean by "authentic offense.")

The *external boundary system* is an invisible and symbolic "fence" that we can use to keep people from coming too close to our bodies and keep us from crowding others physically. The external boundary system has two subparts: the physical and the sexual boundaries. The *physical boundary* protects the nonsexual part of the body. People with intact physical boundaries are able to be physically appropriate with other people and also able to physically protect themselves. The *sexual boundary* is just a more refined aspect of the physical boundary system and protects the sexual parts of the body. People with intact sexual boundaries can be sexually appropriate as well as able to protect them-selves from unwanted or inappropriate sexual advances.

The *internal boundary system* functions like a filter to protect our think-ing, feelings, and behavior. People who have healthy internal boundaries know that they are responsible for what they think, feel, and do, and that no one else makes them think, feel, or do anything. People with impaired internal bound-aries blame others for what they think, feel, or do, and on the other hand they often inappropriately take responsibility for the thoughts, feelings, and behavior of others. People with impaired internal boundaries either can't say no to others and are constantly used or abused, or they put up inflexible walls and can't let *anyone* get close to them emotionally.

People with healthy internal boundaries can choose their own thinking, have their own feelings, and choose to behave the way they need to in order to be in charge of their own well-being and protect themselves. Healthy internal boundaries also allow us to let others have their own thinking, feeling, and behavioral reality, because we know others have that right. And with healthy internal boundaries, we don't get confused about thinking other people's feel-ings and reality are our own.

Intact boundaries protect us when dealing with most people, unless we are dealing with someone who is violent and more powerful physically than we are. But when we have our boundaries in place, we are less likely to be fright-ened or intimidated by people who once had a painful impact on our reality. A boundary system is not only for self-protection, but also to make sure our own behavior stays within functional dimensions so that we do not abuse other people.*

Your boundary system can be in one of five possible conditions: (1) no boundaries, (2) damaged boundaries, (3) a wall around you, (4) vacillation between walls and no boundaries, or (5) intact boundaries. Each part of your boundary system can be in a different condition. For instance, you could have a nonexistent physical boundary, an intact sexual boundary, and a wall around your thinking. In this case, anyone could hit you or push you playfully when you didn't want him or her to, but you could stop the person at once if the contact became sexual. And you could tolerate *no* differences in thinking from the people around you. You would probably walk away from or block out a discussion that might threaten your way of thinking.

The state of powerlessness related to this symptom is this: when you encounter another person in a relationship, you are either unable to defend yourself from abuse and can't say no (no boundaries or damaged ones) or you are so well defended that you have no relationship with anyone (walls). (We will address how you offend others in a later step.)

WHAT TO DO

Use the following chart to assess each part of your boundary system. Note that even though the internal boundary is a single boundary protecting the thinking, feelings, and behavior, for purposes of assessment you will look at each of these separately. Make an X in the appropriate box in each column. For example, if you decide you have nonexistent physical boundaries, place an X in the first box below the heading "External Physical." If you decide you have damaged sexual boundaries, move to the next column, "External Sexual," and put an X in the second box in the column. If you decide your "Internal Thinking" boundary is healthy, mark the box at the bottom of the third column, labeled "Intact."

* A videotape and two audiotapes by Pia Mellody about boundaries are available from Mellody Enterprises, P.O. Box 1739, Wickenburg, AZ 85358.

My Assessment of My Boundary Systems

CONDITION OF BOUNDARY	EXTERNAL PHYSICAL	EXTERNAL SEXUAL	INTERNAL THINKING	INTERNAL FEELING	INTERNAL BEHAVIOR
NO BOUNDARY					
DAMAGED					
WALL: ANGER					
WALL: FEAR					
WALL: SILENCE					
WALL: WORDS					
MOVING FROM NO BOUNDARY TO WALLS					
INTACT (HEALTHY)					

Describe one or more incidents that illustrate how each of your *impaired* boundaries is not intact. By writing down the behaviors you engage in because of your impaired boundaries you can bring your state of powerlessness over this symptom of codependence out of denial and into the open.

EXAMPLE

EXTERNAL SEXUAL BOUNDARY: I believe my sexual boundary is damaged because when I am sick and my mate wants me to be sexual, but it is in my best interest to say no because I am not feeling well, I can't say no. Second, my boundary is damaged because when I want to be sexual and my mate does not, I can't accept his no and I try to force myself on him, whining and pouting or manipulating in other ways until he gives in and is sexual with me.

How My External-Physical Boundary Is Impaired:

How My External-Sexual Boundary Is Impaired:

How My Internal-Thinking Boundary Is Impaired:

How My Internal-Feeling Boundary Is Impaired:

How My Internal-Behavior Boundary Is Impaired:

CORE SYMPTOM 3:
DIFFICULTY OWNING YOUR REALITY

Pages 21–28 in chapter 2 of *Facing Codependence.* Here is a brief summary of the background reading:

Difficulty owning what I call your own "reality" means you have difficulty experiencing who you are and sharing that with other people. The term *reality* refers to the fact that each individual has his or her own unique way of interpreting life. Two people can see the same event and have different thoughts and feelings and decide to do different things because of the event. But the thoughts, feelings, and behavior of each one are *very real* to that person and constitute his or her reality. Your reality comes from within you and mine comes from within me, shaped by the way we respond to our environments as a result of our history.

Your reality includes four areas: (1) knowing what you *look like* and how your body is functioning, (2) understanding and being aware of how you're *thinking,* (3) recognizing and experiencing your *emotions,* and (4) being aware of your *behavior* and its impact on others. Being aware of these four areas gives you a sense of who you are. And recovery is experiencing and sharing your personal environment in a more accurate and less skewed manner in all of these areas.

The core symptom operates at one of two levels:

A. You know what your reality is, but can't or don't share it with anyone.

B. You don't know what your reality is.

Level B is more serious and more dysfunctional.

All four parts of your reality can be experienced at level A or level B. Or with part of your reality you may be healthy, with another part you may be at level A, and with a third part you may be at level B.

The powerlessness related to this symptom is this: you are not able to acknowledge or share one or more of your areas of reality. You are either aware of it but can't acknowledge it to others, or you are totally unaware of what your reality is.

WHAT TO DO

Use the following chart to assess your level of awareness in each area of your reality. Mark an X in the appropriate box in each column. For example, if you find yourself angry at your husband a lot but can't find the courage or the right time to tell him about it, you are at level A with your feeling reality. On the other hand, if you feel emotionally numb even when painful things happen (such as your husband forgets your birthday for the umpteenth time) you are at level B with your feeling reality. If you recognize your emotions and express them when appropriate, you are healthy with your feeling reality.

My Assessment of Owning My Reality

LEVEL OF AWARENESS	PHYSICAL REALITY	THINKING REALITY	FEELING REALITY	BEHAVIORAL REALITY
LEVEL A				
LEVEL B				
HEALTHY				

Level A: Know your reality but can't acknowledge it.

Level B: Don't know what your reality is.

Healthy: Know your reality and can acknowledge it to others when appropriate.

Describe an incident that illustrates your difficulty owning each area of your reality that is at level A or level B. By writing down how you operate at either level A or B with any part of your reality, you can bring your state of powerlessness over this symptom of codependence out of denial and into the open.

EXAMPLE

Body Reality:

I believe I'm at level B with my physical reality because last week everyone in my office thought the air conditioning was turned down too cold and I said I wasn't too cold, but my friends pointed out that my fingernails were light blue and I had goose bumps on my arms.

My Difficulty Owning My Physical Reality

My Difficulty Owning My Thinking Reality

My Difficulty Owning My Feeling Reality

My Difficulty Owning My Behavioral Reality

CORE SYMPTOM 4:
DIFFICULTY ACKNOWLEDGING AND MEETING YOUR NEEDS AND WANTS

BACKGROUND READING

Pages 28–34 in chapter 2 of *Facing Codependence.* Here is a brief summary of the background reading:

This fourth symptom relates to two issues: needs and wants. I use the term *needs* to refer to dependency needs, which are your needs for what you must have to be healthy and survive. They include needs for food, clothing, shelter, physical nurturing, emotional nurturing (time, attention, and direction from other people), medical and dental attention, sexual information and guidance, and financial information and guidance.

Although wants may seem to be less important than needs, they are actually extremely important. It's our wants that bring us joy and take our lives in a decided direction. Without their being met I don't believe we can be fully mature adults.

I divide wants into two categories: little wants and big wants. Little wants are our preferences. They are things we don't have to have, but when we choose them they bring us great joy. Big wants take our lives in a general direction and bring us fulfillment. They include such things as "I want to be married to this person," "I want to be a doctor," "I want to develop this corporation," "I want to have a child."

The symptom of difficulty acknowledging and meeting our own needs and wants is experienced at four levels:

> *I am too dependent:* I know my needs and wants but expect other people to take care of them for me, so I wait for them to do so, not taking care of them myself.

> *I am antidependent:* I am able to acknowledge to myself that I have needs and wants, but I insist on meeting them myself and am unable to accept help or guidance from anyone else. I'd rather go without than be vulnerable and ask for help.

> *I am needless and wantless:* I don't even know that I have needs and wants.

> *I confuse wants with needs:* I know what I want and I get it, but I don't know what I need. I have them backward, so I try to take care of my needs (which I'm unaware of) by trying to get everything I want. But I may miss some very important needs because I have no wants connected with them (for example, going to the doctor or dentist for checkups).

We can be at different levels for each individual need and want. For example, we might be too dependent with emotional nurturing needs, antidependent with big wants, and needless-wantless with physical nurturing needs.

This symptom, like all the others, comes from less-than-nurturing experiences in childhood. The person who is *too dependent* often had almost all his or her needs and wants completely taken care of throughout childhood by the parents. He or she was not taught how to take care of his or her own needs or wants. The person who is *antidependent* often was attacked in childhood whenever he or she expressed a need or want. The person who is *needless-wantless* often was ignored at times of neediness or wanting. The person who *confuses wants with needs* often had parents who did not know how to meet the dependency needs of the child (especially for emotional and physical nurturing) and instead gave the child everything he or she wanted, thinking that would take care of his or her needs.

The powerlessness related to this symptom is this: you have difficulty acknowledging and taking care of your own needs and wants in one or more of four ways. You are aware of them but expect others to take care of them for you; or you meet certain ones yourself but cannot ask for help in meeting others, so you do without; or you do not know that you have certain needs and wants; or you may try to meet your needs by getting things you want, but your needs are still unmet.

WHAT TO DO

Use the following checklists to evaluate where you are with each of the major dependency needs. Then mark an X in the appropriate box in each column of the chart on page 54.

FOOD

Do I eat three nourishing, well-balanced meals a day?

Do I eat the proper quantities?

Do I know how to cook well enough to provide for myself?

Do I know how to order properly balanced foods in restaurants?

Do I follow any special food advice I have received from my doctor in relation to special needs my body has (for example, high cholesterol, excess weight, blood pressure, diabetes, heart condition)?

CLOTHING

Do I take care of my clothes, keeping them clean and mended?

Do my clothes fit me properly, being neither too tight nor too baggy?

Do I have enough appropriate clothes to wear to my job or for social occasions?

Am I confident about choosing what to wear to any occasion?

SHELTER

Is my neighborhood safe and appropriate for me?

Do I live in a secure dwelling with adequate space?

Am I comfortable having friends visit me where I live?

Do I have appropriate furniture?

Is my home in fairly good repair (paint, plumbing, knobs on cabinets, door knobs, and so on)?

Are the walls decorated pleasantly?

Do I keep my living space reasonably clean and orderly?

Do I have the necessary equipment to care for myself and my home (for example, kitchen implements, cleaning equipment, grooming equipment for myself)?

PHYSICAL NURTURING

When I need a hug, can I go to an appropriate person and ask for one?

When I am tired and no one is around to hug me, can I go and get a massage or sit in a hot tub or lie down and rest to take care of myself physically?

EMOTIONAL NURTURING

Do I have safe friends from whom I can get time, attention, and direction?

Do I go to those friends for time, attention, direction, and to share my reality?

Do I limit my expectations to sharing my reality and receiving nurturing, not expecting them to fix me up or meet my needs or wants unless I ask directly for help?

Do I ask for information about things I don't know about when the need arises (for example, how to balance a checkbook, how to make an airline reservation, where to get my car fixed, how to fill out my income tax return)?

MEDICAL/DENTAL ATTENTION

Do I have regular physical checkups?

Do I have my teeth cleaned and checked on a regular basis?

Do I respond to real physical problems by going to the doctor?

Do I follow doctors' instructions reasonably well?

SEXUAL INFORMATION AND GUIDANCE

Do I have sex only with an appropriate partner (spouse, significant other)?

Can I say no to my partner when necessary to take care of me?

Do I know what turns me on and what turns me off?

Can I communicate these things to my partner?

Can I say no to inappropriate sexual offers?

If I have no partner, do I know how to meet my own sexual needs through masturbation or some other way?

FINANCIAL INFORMATION AND GUIDANCE

Do I spend within my means?

Am I self-supporting (as opposed to relying on parents or other outside help on a continuing basis)?

Do I budget my financial resources?

Do I do the necessary record keeping to be aware of what I need financially?

Do I earn enough to meet my needs for food, shelter, clothing, medical/dental services, and financial security (savings)?

Do I pay my bills on time?

Do I report my income and expenses honestly?

Do I buy what is reasonably priced and of reasonable quality (as opposed to buying inferior items or lavish ones)?

Use the following chart to evaluate where you are with both your little and big wants. Place an X in the appropriate box in each column.

My Assessment of How I Meet Needs

Level of Functioning	Food	Clothing	Shelter	Physical Nurturing	Emotional Nurturing	Medical/ Dental Attention	Sexual Info. & Guidance	Financial Info. & Guidance
Too dependent								
Anti-dependent								
Needless/ wantless								
Confuse needs with wants								
Healthy								

Too dependent: I know I have needs but I don't acknowledge or take care of them.

Antidependent: I know I have needs but I do not or cannot ask for help.

Needless: I am unaware I have needs.

Confuse needs with wants: I take care of needs (of which I am unaware) by getting what I want (which I can recognize).

Healthy: I acknowledge and meet my needs.

My Assessment of How I Meet Wants

LEVEL OF FUNCTIONING	LITTLE WANTS (PREFERENCES)	BIG WANTS (AFFECTING LIFE GOALS)
TOO DEPENDENT		
ANTIDEPENDENT		
WANTLESS		
CONFUSE WANTS WITH NEEDS		
HEALTHY		

Too dependent: I know what I want but expect others to meet my wants.

Antidependent: I know what I want but do not or cannot ask for help.

Wantless: I don't know what I want.

Confuse wants with needs: I get wants met in an attempt to meet needs.

Healthy: I acknowledge my wants and meet them.

Describe specific incidents that illustrate your difficulty meeting the kinds of needs and wants you evaluated in the two previous charts. By writing down specific examples of the behaviors you engage in as a result of this difficulty, you can bring your state of powerlessness over this symptom of codependence out of denial and into the open.

My Difficulty Meeting My Needs

My Difficulty Meeting My Needs

My Difficulty Meeting My Wants

CORE SYMPTOM 5:
DIFFICULTY EXPERIENCING AND EXPRESSING
YOUR REALITY MODERATELY

BACKGROUND READING

Pages 35–42 in chapter 2 of *Facing Codependence*. Here is a brief summary of the background reading:

This fifth symptom pervades the whole disease of codependence. It can be referred to as "the either/or syndrome" and is sometimes described as the feeling that we have no rheostats about our reality. We express our reality extremely (either no expression or crisislike eruptions) in each of the four areas of reality: physical, thinking, feelings, and behavior.

THE BODY

Many codependents dress immoderately—either wearing tight skimpy clothing or clothes that are layered or so baggy and shapeless that the body's shape is concealed from the observer. Or the person wears clothes marked by bright colors or extreme design so that every head turns when the person enters a room. At the opposite extreme is clothing that is so bland and ordinary the person is practically invisible in a group.

Regarding body size, a person may gain a lot of weight until his or her true body shape is hidden by fat. On the other hand, the person might starve himself or herself so that the true body shape is distorted by thinness and therefore hidden. This core issue is often expressed through an eating disorder such as compulsive overeating and/or bulimia, which is an illness involving overeating followed by purging and starving. I find many sexually abused people with eating disorders, and I believe the disorders are related to this core issue of difficulty expressing one's physical reality moderately and at the appropriate age level.

Codependents may also have trouble dressing appropriately for their age. A young woman may dress in clothes far too mature for her age—somber colors, severely tailored clothes, or clothes that look "frumpy" on such a young person. In fact, people who see her may estimate that she is ten to fifteen years older than she really is. At the other extreme is a middle-aged woman dressing in the current styles of her teenage daughter and wearing her hair in a style that younger women or young girls wear.

THINKING

Codependents often come up with skewed interpretations of what is going on around them and develop extreme solutions to problems.

A person with this difficulty can easily interpret someone's complimentary remark as a sarcastic criticism, or someone's humor as a painful attack. "Solutions" arrived at on the basis of skewed interpretations often have the codependent doing exactly the opposite of whatever he or she thinks is causing the problem. For instance, if a man's wife tells him that she would appreciate it if he wouldn't interrupt her so often when she's working on the bookkeeping, he might decide NEVER to interrupt her and not to tell her about telephone calls or even genuine emergencies she needs to be informed about. Or if a husband asks his wife to spend a little less on the groceries, she might decide to put the whole family on basic survival rations in order to avoid overspending on the food.

FEELINGS

Difficulty experiencing and expressing our feelings with moderation and at our own age level is almost a given for any codependent in touch with the shame core. This difficulty with moderation is also automatic with any codependent whose internal boundaries are so impaired that the feeling reality of other people is easily absorbed. Most codependents express feeling reality very immoderately, either having no awareness of feelings (frozen feelings) or experiencing strong, overwhelming feelings. We come across to others as either very immature and chaotic or supermature and tightly self-controlled (and controlling).

A codependent adult may experience at least four different kinds of feeling reality:

Adult feeling reality: You experience a mature emotional response to your thinking that does not dredge up data from the past. You feel centered when you experience it.

Adult-to-adult induced feeling reality: You take on emotions from other adults. This can happen when you are physically close to someone who is feeling intensely, is in denial of his or her feelings, or is acting irresponsibly with his or her feelings. This experience is called *empathy* when the amount taken on is moderate and controlled by the internal boundary. When too much feeling is taken on, you feel overwhelmed and crazy.

Frozen feelings from childhood: You experience the release of your own feeings from childhood that were not safe to feel as a child. To survive whatever abuse you experienced, you shut down or "froze" the feelings. As you begin to come out of your defense mechanism, you feel these feelings as an adult. You feel extremely vulnerable and childlike when you experience them.

Carried or induced feelings from childhood: You feel the feelings of the person who abused you that were induced into you in childhood. You feel overwhelmed or out of control when you experience them.

BEHAVIOR

A person who trusts everyone or no one at all has difficulty with moderate behavior. So does a person who either doesn't defend himself or herself at all or repeats his or her parent's offending behavior. For example, this person might beat his or her children because that's what Dad did, or go to the other extreme out of dislike for what Dad did and never discipline them at all.

THE SOURCE OF THIS SYMPTOM

I believe extreme expressions of all four areas of reality (physical, thinking, feeling, and behavioral) come from observing our major caregivers expressing their own reality immoderately. In addition, codependents experience feelings at extreme levels because they encounter four different kinds of feeling realities: adult feeling reality, adult-induced feeling reality, frozen feelings from childhood, and adult-to-child carried feelings.

The powerlessness related to this symptom is this: the way your reality feels to you and also the way you express it to others is extreme. Your distorted reality can feel very painful to you, or its expression to others can be extremely offensive and explosive. Or your communication of it can be the opposite — subdued or withheld altogether. You may operate immoderately in only one or two areas, or you may operate immoderately in different ways in each area.

WHAT TO DO

Describe one or more incidents that illustrate how you have difficulty experiencing and/or expressing your reality with moderation and at your own age level in any or all parts of your reality. By writing down specific examples of your ways of experiencing and expressing your reality to extreme degrees you can bring your state of powerlessness over this symptom of codependence out of denial and into the open.

My Difficulty Experiencing and Expressing My Physical Reality Moderately

My Difficulty Experiencing and Expressing My Thinking Reality Moderately

My Difficulty Experiencing and Expressing My Feeling Reality Moderately

My Difficulty with Moderate Behavior

Unmanageable Consequences of the Five Core Symptoms

These exercises are designed to help you see more clearly what is unmanageable in your life due to codependence. Describing how the symptoms are sabotaging your relationships and affecting the flow of your everyday existence will help you move beyond denial – even beyond the general admission of "Yes, my life is unmanageable and I'm miserable"– and into awareness.

I believe that each core symptom creates unmanageable or harmful consequences. In other words, I believe that the unmanageable consequences in your life are created when you are in a state of powerlessness, experiencing one or more of the five core symptoms. *Unmanageable consequences follow powerlessness.*

I have identified at least five kinds of unmanageable consequences: negative control, resentment, distorted or nonexistent spirituality, avoiding reality, and impaired intimacy. Often a single consequence can be caused by several different core symptoms operating at once. In other words, the unmanageable consequences are not directly related to any single symptom.

Complete the suggested background reading before you write about each consequence. Read about one consequence at a time, then do the writing about that consequence before reading about the next one. Don't worry if you need to spend a month or longer on each one. As your denial, minimization, and delusion gradually recede, you will be able to write more.

CONSEQUENCE 1: NEGATIVE CONTROL

BACKGROUND READING

Pages 44–47 in chapter 4 of *Facing Codependence.* Here is a brief summary of the background reading:

Codependents primarily live in constant reaction to others rather than instigating action for themselves, and as a result they get involved in controlling or determining other people's reality in order to feel safe and comfortable. I call it negative control whenever you give yourself permission to determine what another person's reality is to be. You do this when you tell a person what he or she should look like (the body), what meaning he or she is to give incoming data (thinking), what emotions he or she should be having (feeling), or what he or she should do or not do (behavior). On the other hand, you are also involved in negative control when you give someone else permission to determine what you should look like, how you should interpret incoming data, what you should feel, and what you should do or not do.

Positive control involves your determining your own reality apart and distinct from the reality of others. You establish for yourself what you're going to look like, think, feel, do, and not do. You are in control of your reality, of knowing what it is, embracing it, and expressing it when it's in your best interest to do so. Positive control is recovery—the opposite of negative control.

There are three exceptions to the general definition of negative control I just gave. First, when we are parents, we must engage in influencing a child's reality. This may look like negative control on the surface, but when it's done respectfully, moderately, and with good reason, it isn't negative control.

Second, when you hire a therapist, you are buying the therapist's ability to influence your reality. It could appear to be negative control, but because that is clearly the purpose of therapy, it is excluded from the category of unhealthy negative control.

And third, when you ask someone (such as a sponsor or a friend) for his or her opinion about your reality, that person has permission to tell you. This instance does not represent negative control because the person has your permission to influence your reality by his or her opinion.

Writing about your experiences with negative control and describing the negative control behaviors you engage in brings your experience of unmanageable consequences out of denial.

WHAT TO DO

Describe instances when you have engaged in negative control by determining someone else's reality.

EXAMPLE

When Sammy, my son, came home angry at his friend, Bobby, I told him nice boys don't get angry over things like that. I did not allow him to feel his own feelings or guide him in the healthy expression of them.

When my husband said that he wanted to go to McDonald's for his birthday dinner, I told him he really didn't want to go there. I told him he wanted to go to a fancier restaurant.

How I Have Engaged in Negative Control by Controlling Others

Describe instances in which you have engaged in negative control by allowing others to determine your reality when it was not in your best interest to do so.

EXAMPLE	I decided I needed to see the dentist because I had a toothache. My wife stated that it was not a bad toothache and that I should not go see the dentist. I thought she was wrong, but followed her direction. My tooth abscessed three weeks later.

How I Have Engaged in Negative Control by Letting Others Control Me

CONSEQUENCE 2: RESENTMENT

BACKGROUND READING

Pages 47–50 in chapter 3 of *Facing Codependence.*

Here is more information about resentment.

Resentment seems to come from your perception that someone has committed an injurious act against you. The event could have been an authentic act of offense or an incident in which your value system clashed with someone else's, although the other person did not transgress your boundaries. It doesn't really matter which one it is. You are likely to experience resentment as a result of either one.

The resentment process involves obsessively thinking about what happened. A pattern develops in which you first recall the incident, which generates anger. Next, out of the anger you focus on ways to get revenge or to punish the perpetrator. You are motivated toward revenge or punishment by a two-part mistaken belief: (1) that getting even or punishing the wrongdoer will control his or her behavior and keep such incidents from ever happening again and (2) that the guilty party's suffering will restore your sense of worth that you believe was lost because of the injurious incident.

Resentments dating back to incidents that happened in childhood are another category altogether. I believe that these need to be addressed in therapy and not in this section of the workbook.

WHAT TO DO

In the column on the left, describe incidents about which you have been resentful (or are still resentful). (REMINDER: Do not include childhood resentments.) Then, in the column on the right, describe your thoughts about ways to get revenge or punish the perpetrator.

EXAMPLE

INCIDENT CAUSING RESENTMENT	WHAT I HAVE DONE TO CONTROL THE SITUATION, TRYING TO PROTECT MYSELF
My roommate's parakeet lives free in our house. She enjoys the parakeet's company and seeing it fly free. But she doesn't clean up the mess the bird makes. I resent living with the mess or having to clean it up.	I whine and complain to her about the mess. I explain in an angry voice that I am *not* going to live with this filth, I hate having to clean up the mess, and she'd better do something about that parakeet or else! Each day that goes by and she doesn't change, I get more angry, thinking that if I can make her miserable enough, she will take better care of the parakeet and our house.

My Experience with Resentment

INCIDENT CAUSING RESENTMENT	WHAT I HAVE DONE TO CONTROL THE SITUATION, TRYING TO PROTECT MYSELF

A HEALTHIER RESPONSE

A healthy response to experiencing such hurtful events is to understand and accept that it happened and is beyond your control, do what you can do to protect yourself, turn it over to the Higher Power using Step Three, and go on with your life without obsessively thinking about the event and having resentment.

Empowering yourself in a healthy way involves taking action for yourself *without* involving the person whom you resent. Your thinking moves from "You've got to change so I can get over my resentment. You have the power in this situation," to "This is the problem that I'm having as a result of being in a relationship with this person. What can I do to resolve the issue that doesn't involve him or her?" In the case of authentic offenses that are likely to recur, you need to tell the offender what his or her offending behavior is and that you would like for it to stop. But keep in mind that you cannot make a person do or not do anything. If the offense happens again, take steps to reduce your contact with the person to protect yourself.

When you can make a decision in your own best interest to resolve the situation without involving the other person, you wind up feeling empowered again and able to take care of yourself, and the resentment caused by feeling powerless often goes away.

In the column on the left, briefly describe each resentment you listed in the previous exercise. Then, in the column on the right, choose one of the following three options:

1. Describe as many options you can think of that do not involve change on the part of the person you resent.

2. Acknowledge this as a situation for which there is no plan you can think of that does not involve the other person's changing. Be very careful before making this selection. Check with other people in recovery (your therapist, your sponsor, people in meetings) about whether they can see options you may not have thought of. Denial and old thinking patterns can make it difficult to see options clearly. In situations like this, the way out of resentment is to give up knowing how relief can come and prepare to turn it over to a Higher Power. We will discuss how Step Three helps us do this later in the workbook.

3. Describe how this situation is a case of you being actively offended by another adult. For example, someone may be physically attacking you, attacking your thinking by ridiculing it or demeaning it, or exploiting your emotional reality by deliberately using your fears or areas of pain to manipulate you.

If this is the situation regarding this resentment, use your anger to give you the energy to take care of yourself. Begin by describing in the column on the right what you can say to this person about what is happening, what emotions you are feeling, and what you would like for the person to do differently. Realize that you can only ask for what you want, you cannot *make* a person change. If the person does not change, describe what you can do to reduce contact with this person to take care of yourself.

EXAMPLE

Situation number 1: Clash of value systems

INCIDENT CAUSING RESENTMENT	NEW OPTIONS I CAN TAKE
My roommate's parakeet makes messes. I resent cleaning them up.	Hire a housekeeper to clean up the mess. Buy a cage and put the parakeet in it.

EXAMPLE

Situation number 2: Clash of value systems, but there is no acceptable plan that does not involve the other person.

INCIDENT CAUSING RESENTMENT	NEW OPTIONS I CAN TAKE
When my children from an earlier marriage visit me, my wife becomes angry because they monopolize the living room and the television. She doesn't like what they like to watch, and they don't like to watch her programs. I resent her attitude toward my children.	I see that it is irritating to have young teenagers take over the living space that belongs to her as well as to me. I will not stop having my kids visit, so I can only acknowledge my anger and resentment while giving up having to know how the situation will be resolved.*

* After this man gave up trying to solve this situation and stopped obsessively focusing on ways to change his wife's attitude, his wife came up with the idea of building a room on their house in which she could be comfortable while his children were visiting. Since they had the money, they built it, but the man did not insist that his wife give up her claim to their joint living room, nor did he stop having his children visit. I realize not everyone could solve the problem this way, but it is surprising how solutions come even when we can't think of what they might be.

EXAMPLE

Situation number 3

INCIDENT CAUSING RESENTMENT	NEW OPTIONS I CAN TAKE
When I tell my boyfriend about my plans to start a child care service in my home, he tells me that I don't know anything about business and I'm so scatterbrained I could never learn. He lectures me about how I'll just get into trouble because I'm not smart enough to deal with all the details. I resent his attacking my intellectual ability and feel anger and pain as well.	I now recognize this as an act of intellectual offense on my boyfriend's part. I need to tell him that when he criticizes my thinking ability without really knowing whether I can do these things or not I feel anger and pain. I will ask him not to be critical of my intellectual ability when I talk to him about this plan. If he continues to criticize my thinking, I can stop talking to him about the plan and find people to talk to who can be more supportive. I can also evaluate whether I want to continue a relationship in which I am attacked like this.

My Experience with Healthy Options

INCIDENT CAUSING RESENTMENT	*NEW OPTIONS I CAN CHOOSE*

CONSEQUENCE 3:
DISTORTED OR NONEXISTENT SPIRITUALITY

BACKGROUND READING

Pages 50–54 in chapter 4 of *Facing Codependence.* Here is a brief summary of the background reading plus some additional information:*

Two unmanageable consequences fall under this heading: (1) difficulty sharing who we are with others and hearing who they are, and (2) difficulty experiencing a power greater than ourselves.

Many people seem to believe that the closer to perfection we get, the more spiritual we are. A similar belief is that we must be perfect in order to be assured of getting into heaven. But any belief that we must not have any imperfections to be acceptable to God and to others is one of the ways our spirituality is distorted. The belief is accompanied by the conviction that it is we ourselves who must achieve perfection, and that whenever any imperfection is apparent, there is something we are not doing right in our spiritual lives.

In my opinion, this belief can bring about real difficulty owning our own imperfection and being accountable for it when it hurts someone else. This form of skewed spirituality contributes to our loss of awareness of our reality (thinking, feeling, behavioral, and physical reality) because anything that is not judged to be perfect (or "spiritual" in the distorted sense) is unacceptable and must be put away from us somehow (hidden). Believing that a human being can ever be perfect is part of a codependent's skewed thinking reality.

In addition, people following this belief that spirituality is perfection become involved in judging and comparing themselves to other people. Deciding how well people are doing and how "spiritual" they are begins to take up more and more mental and emotional energy. Judging who is better and who is worse is a part of codependence stemming from inappropriate levels of self-esteem and the unmanageable consequence of negative control, as we have seen.

I believe that whenever we can't embrace our own imperfection, we are not open to experiencing spirituality. Either we believe that we are perfect (or deny that we are imperfect), which results in acting as our own Higher Power. Or we may believe that we are abnormally imperfect, which results in not being able to stand sharing our imperfection with ourselves or anyone else because it's so awful we are convinced that people will go away if we tell them, and a Higher Power would not accept us either.

Along these same lines, when we are not able to accept that other people are imperfect, we obstruct our own spiritual experience. When we hear someone else share his or her imperfection with us, or that person's imperfection causes trouble for us we either (1) try to exert negative control over that per-

---

* A four-cassette lecture by Pia Mellody about spirituality is available from Mellody Enterprises, P.O. Box 1739, Wickenburg, AZ 85358.

son to change his or her imperfection or (2) experience inordinate amounts of pain and anger leading to judgment and resentment. There is an appropriate level of pain and anger when someone hurts us. But the acceptance of imperfection in others can help lessen the degree and duration of such feelings and help us avoid judging and resenting them.

Some people approach the recovery process with the hope that it will help them stop being "crazy" and out of touch with their identity and teach them how to be perfect. This search for a way to be and do perfectly is part of our skewed thinking reality.

HOW SPIRITUALITY FREES US TO OWN OUR IMPERFECTIONS

Human beings are imperfect to some degree and to various levels of seriousness. There is no getting away from our imperfection — ever. This is the normal condition of a functional, healthy human being and is why we need a Higher Power. I call this condition "perfectly imperfect," being aware and accepting of our imperfections while still trying to deal with and change hurtful character defects.

In my opinion accepting that we are imperfect allows us to see more clearly that the power we need to surmount these imperfections is not a human power but a spiritual one greater than and outside of ourselves. Further, as long as the imperfection persists, we can admit to ourselves that we have value even when we are imperfect and have joy about our value, but we also can have pain when we know that our imperfection causes trouble for us and for others in relationship with us. In addition we need to love and accept others as having value when they are imperfect, protecting ourselves where necessary but avoiding judgment and criticism of them.

HOW SPIRITUALITY BRINGS US INTO CONTACT WITH OUR HIGHER POWER

When we can embrace this normal condition of perfect imperfection in ourselves, share it with someone else, and hear someone else share his or hers, we are open to the experience of spirituality. Often it is the very moment we become aware that an imperfection has been operating in our lives that we simultaneously experience being connected to a Higher Power. At other times, when we tell someone else about our imperfection and are heard without judgment by the other person, we are also open to contact with the Higher Power. And moments in which we do not judge someone as we hear his or her imperfection offer opportunities for this spiritual experience. At such moments, we experience pain from the awareness of the imperfection, accompanied by joy about the spiritual connectedness and the fact that we have value while we are imperfect. The emotion becomes either joy-filled pain or pain-filled joy, depending on which emotion is greater at the moment.

WHAT TO DO

In the column on the left, describe the ways in which you have difficulty relating to a Higher Power. Then, in the column on the right, list the core symptom(s) from which the difficulty is coming.

Describing the difficulty you have in relating to a Higher Power brings your experience of this unmanageable consequence out of denial and into the open.

EXAMPLE		
	DIFFICULTY RELATING TO A HIGHER POWER	*CORE SYMPTOM(S) INVOLVED*
	I am afraid of a higher power because I think if I reveal my imperfections I will be attacked and punished.	When I think about my imperfections, I feel so much shame. My level of *self-esteem* is so low that I can't believe a Higher Power would be interested in restoring me to sanity.

My Difficulty Relating to a Higher Power

DIFFICULTY RELATING TO A HIGHER POWER	CORE SYMPTOM(S) INVOLVED

In the column on the left, describe ways in which you avoid acknowledging your own imperfection. Then, in the column on the right, name the core symptom(s) from which your fear of sharing your imperfection or your lack of awareness of your imperfection comes.

Describing your difficulty sharing imperfection with someone brings your experience of this unmanageable consequence out of denial and into the open.

EXAMPLE	*WAYS I HIDE IMPERFECTION*	*CORE SYMPTOM(S) INVOLVED*
	I told my husband I'd meet him at home for lunch, but when noon came, I suddenly remembered I'd promised to have lunch with a friend. I rushed off to lunch and forgot to call my husband, who went home and fixed both of us a lunch. After I got back to the office I remembered and called home. I lied and told him I had tried to call him beforehand but he hadn't been home (I knew he had gone to an appointment before lunch).	I have difficulty owning my own reality and rely on certain key people to give it to me. I could not tell my husband I had forgotten about the lunch appointment until too late to call him and that I had forgotten to call from the restaurant where I met my friend. I wanted him to think I had tried to get in touch with him because his opinion of me is my reality about myself.

My Difficulty Acknowledging Imperfection

WAYS I HIDE IMPERFECTION	CORE SYMPTOM(S) INVOLVED

CONSEQUENCE 4: AVOIDING REALITY

Pages 52–54 in chapter 3 of *Facing Codependence.* Here is a brief summary of the background reading:

As a result of experiencing abuse in childhood, adult codependents try to avoid "intolerable" reality. But even if you try to avoid the reality, it is within you anyway. You know and feel about it, and if you are aware you know, you've known and felt about it before.

As I've said, codependents are immature people in adult bodies who often have difficulty functioning as mature adults. These conditions mean that your life is filled with stress and feeling reality that is difficult to deal with.

I believe that codependents experience one or more of the following three ways of medicating or removing this reality from consciousness: an addictive process, physical illness, and mental illness.

ADDICTIONS AND CODEPENDENCE

I believe that for many people, addictions are an outgrowth of core symptoms of codependence. An addiction can form around any process that relieves intolerable reality. Because of the relief an addictive substance or behavior brings, it becomes a priority in your life, taking time and attention away from other priorities. And this growing absorption leads to harmful consequences in your relationships that you choose to ignore. You learn to medicate your unwanted reality through one or more addictive processes. The ones you choose are the ones that relieve the intolerable reality in the most acceptable, efficient way for you.

PHYSICAL ILLNESS AND CODEPENDENCE

If your need to control reality is great and you don't indulge in an addiction, your unacknowledged and unmedicated feelings will be expressed in some form. The *Diagnostic and Statistical Manual of Mental Disorders* (DSM) refers to these physical expressions of stress as *somataform disorders.* These are chronic physical symptoms that a doctor can never fully treat and bring relief from. Many people come up with one physical illness after another. I believe many of these symptoms are produced by the stress of the codependent's avoiding the pain of owning his or her own reality and not learning to appropriately experience and express his or her feeling reality.

MENTAL ILLNESS AND CODEPENDENCE

The reality of what happened to you in childhood can be extremely traumatizing and horrible. In order to survive, you, as a child, had to keep yourself from fully knowing about and having feelings about that reality. Later, when using mental illness to protect yourself from knowing, you take your pain outside the realm of conscious mental reality so that you don't have to deal with what is or was. When you are outside the realm of reality, what happened to you for all intents and purposes doesn't exist, and if it did it doesn't matter.

WHAT TO DO

In the column on the left, describe any addictions you have engaged in. Then, in the column on the right, name the core symptom(s) driving this addiction. Describing your addictions and the core symptoms that drive them will bring your avoidance of reality out of denial.

EXAMPLE		
	ADDICTION	*CORE SYMPTOM(S) INVOLVED*
	Compulsive overeating	Low self-esteem, shame Lack of boundaries Difficulty owning my feelings
	Workaholism	Arrogance and grandiosity Lack of boundaries Antidependence—cannot ask for help
	Drug addiction	Low self-esteem Difficulty owning my feelings
	Sex addiction	Low self-esteem Lack of boundaries Inability to be moderate
	Love addiction	Low self-esteem Lack of boundaries Inability to take care of my adult needs and wants

Addictions I Use to Avoid Reality

ADDICTION	CORE SYMPTOM(S) INVOLVED

In the left column, describe any physical symptoms you currently experience that have resisted traditional medical treatment. Then, in the right column, name the core symptom(s) you believe may be behind the physical symptom. Describing your chronic physical symptoms and the core symptoms to which they may be connected will help bring your avoidance of reality out of denial.

EXAMPLE	CHRONIC PHYSICAL SYMPTOM	CORE SYMPTOM(S) INVOLVED*
	Sinus infection—head hurts so bad I have to go to bed	Antidependence—I can't ask for help, get overwhelmed with too much to do.
	Neck muscle pain	Difficulty owning my reality—I hold in pain and fear but "shoulder" my responsibilities without complaining.
	Chronic constipation	Using walls instead of boundaries—I protect myself with walls out of fear of being open and trusting. I hold in my reality behind the wall and end up constipated.

* At first you may need help in making the connection between your chronic physical symptoms and the specific core symptom involved. But it is surprising how often your "guesses" will be true. So give it your best try and check later with your sponsor or others in the recovery process.

Physical Symptoms I Use to Avoid Reality

CHRONIC PHYSICAL SYMPTOM	CORE SYMPTOM(S) INVOLVED

In the left column, describe any mental conditions you currently experience (such as depression, delusion, psychotic episodes). Then, in the right column, name the core symptom(s) to which you believe these conditions may be linked. Describing your mental conditions and the core symptoms that are involved brings your avoidance of reality out of denial.

EXAMPLE

MENTAL CONDITIONS	CORE SYMPTOM(S) INVOLVED
Depression, comes and goes	Difficulty owning my reality—my unnamed emotions of shame, anger, pain, and fear strain for release.
Frequent anxiety attacks	Difficulty owning my reality of imperfection. Fear of not doing it "right."

Mental Conditions I Use to Avoid Reality

MENTAL CONDITION	CORE SYMPTOM(S) INVOLVED

CONSEQUENCE 5: IMPAIRED ABILITY TO SUSTAIN INTIMATE RELATIONSHIPS

BACKGROUND READING

Pages 54–56 in chapter 3 of *Facing Codependence.* Here is a brief summary of the background reading:

One of the hallmarks of codependence is that we have difficulty in relationships with others (and with ourselves and God). Intimacy means that I can share myself with you because I feel good about myself and I can let you share yourself with me without trying to change who you are. Intimacy also involves an exchange. One person is giving and the other is receiving. Sometimes both occur at once. For example, a hug presents two ways to be intimate. (1) When I say to you, "Can I give you a hug?" I am approaching you and nurturing you. (2) When I say, "Would you give me a hug?" I am asking you to approach me and be intimate with me. During the hug both of us are being physically intimate, but one is giving and one is receiving.

Intimacy with someone can be experienced in these ways:

Physical Intimacy:	sharing the *body* in a nurturing, nonsexual manner.
Sexual Intimacy:	sharing the *body* in a sexual manner
Intellectual Intimacy:	sharing *thinking* or thoughts, perceptions
Emotional Intimacy:	sharing *feelings*
Behavioral Intimacy:	sharing what you have *done or not done*

WHAT TO DO

In the column on the left, review each type of intimacy (physical, sexual, intellectual, emotional, behavioral) and write about any that you are unable to share with others with whom you are in relationship (spouse or significant other, child, parent, friends). Then, in the column on the right, name the core symptom(s) to which your difficulty is related.

Describing your own difficulty sharing intimately with others and receiving intimately from others brings your experience of this unmanageable consequence out of denial.

EXAMPLE

AREA OF REALITY I HAVE DIFFICULTY SHARING	CORE SYMPTOM(S) INVOLVED
The body: I am embarrassed for my husband to see me undressed because I need to lose weight. I'm afraid he'll be turned off and leave me. We are sexual in the dark and I always keep my body covered up.	Low self-esteem (worth gained from condition of body) Impaired external boundaries: wall of fear Difficulty owning my physical reality and sharing it (level A)
Thinking: I compare my thinking to yours and judge yours better and mine not worth sharing.	Low self-esteem Difficulty owning my thinking reality (level A)
Feelings: I either hold in my feelings to "spare you" or blast you with them uncontrollably.	Impaired internal boundaries Difficulty owning my emotional reality (level A) Difficulty expressing my reality moderately
Behavior: I feel worthless whenever I make a mistake, so I never admit when I've made one.	Low self-esteem Difficulty owning my behavioral reality

My Difficulty with Expressing Intimacy

AREA OF REALITY I HAVE DIFFICULTY SHARING	CORE SYMPTOM(S) INVOLVED

In the column on the left, review each type of intimacy (physical, sexual, intellectual, emotional, and behavioral) and describe ways in which you have difficulty receiving intimately from each person with whom you are in relationship (spouse or significant other, child, parent, friends). Then, in the column on the right, name the core symptom(s) to which your difficulty is related.

EXAMPLE	
AREA OF REALITY I HAVE DIFFICULTY RECEIVING	**CORE SYMPTOM(S) INVOLVED**
The body: When my wife offers to hug me, I refuse because I fear getting that close to her.	Impaired boundaries
Thinking: When my son thinks of a better idea about how to repair the car, I tell him his idea is stupid so he doesn't look smarter than I am.	Low self-esteem
Feelings: When my wife (or anyone else) starts crying, I can't stand to be in the room with her or discuss anything until she stops crying.	Impaired internal boundary (nonexistent boundaries)
Behavior: I judge and criticize what my adult daughter does, wanting her to do things my way, which I know is better.	Inappropriate level of self-esteem (arrogance and grandiosity) Impaired internal boundary (damaged boundary—I don't do this with others)

My Difficulty with Receiving Intimacy

AREA OF REALITY I HAVE DIFFICULTY RECEIVING	CORE SYMPTOM(S) INVOLVED

Step Two

PURPOSE OF EXERCISE

Step Two addresses your issues of imperfection and your spiritual connection to a Higher Power. As I said in the previous section, to relate to a higher power in a healthy way that leads to recovery, you must be able to view yourself as being what I call "perfectly imperfect" and still value or esteem yourself.

Problems concerning spirituality and a relationship to a Higher Power come up immediately in Step Two. The goal of this step is to correct any skewed thinking you may have about (1) whether there is a Higher Power, (2) how it will respond to you if you turn to it, and (3) whether you need to be restored to sanity. This is the process of coming to believe that a power greater than yourself (and greater than your parents) can restore you to sanity. To me, the sanity to which codependents must be restored is the knowledge that we are perfectly imperfect, that we can only do certain things about that, and that imperfection is the normal human condition.

BACKGROUND READING

Pages 181–189 in chapter 14 of *Facing Codependence*.

Here is a summary of what I believe to be the common problems codependents have with relating to a Higher Power:

Three basic stances toward a Higher Power seem to be set up by the experience of growing up in a dysfunctional family. Some people have a blend of two or all three of them.

1. *There is no Higher Power; I am my own Higher Power.* Two experiences a child can have in a dysfunctional family can set this up. The first is when parents abandon the child and never confront or correct the child's imperfection. The child gets the message that anything he or

93

she wants to do or say is acceptable. There is no Higher Power to guide and correct such a child in these matters. On becoming an adult, the person doesn't really understand that he or she has any imperfection. Therefore, there is no place for a Higher Power in the adult person's life because the person is his or her own Higher Power. Further, such a person doesn't feel a need to be restored to sanity because the person doesn't know that he or she has any insanity.

The second experience that can create this attitude toward the Higher Power is when parents enmesh with the child and manipulate him or her into taking care of them or their responsibilities, instead of taking care of the child and leaving him or her free to be a child. The message from the parent is that the child is the Higher Power of the parent, of the family, and of himself or herself. Therefore, on becoming an adult this person has great difficulty grasping at an operational level the idea that there is a Higher Power, having BEEN the Higher Power of others and of himself or herself since childhood.

2. *A Higher Power exists but isn't there for me.* This attitude is usually that of the child who was ignored in childhood. The parent was minimally involved with the child concerning a few dependency needs and wants, but not enough to teach the child how to acknowledge or take care of these needs and wants. This child, on becoming an adult and considering the concept of a Higher Power, believes that a Higher Power exists but won't restore him or her to sanity. The person cannot turn to a Higher Power for help or strength in any real sense because he or she expects to be ignored.

3. *The Higher Power is harsh, punitive, and critical. The process of being restored to sanity will be shaming, painful, and miserable.* This is usually the attitude of the child who was attacked with criticism and punishment when he or she was imperfect. In adulthood this person might believe that there's a power greater than himself or herself that will restore the person to sanity, but doesn't believe that it's going to be comfortable or that life will be any better. The person has a negative relationship with a Higher Power and cannot embrace or share any issues of his or her own imperfection. To avoid being attacked, this person has great difficulty talking about his or her imperfection to anybody or admitting his or her imperfections to a Higher Power.

This reaction can sometimes lead to actually denying that a Higher Power even exists so that the whole issue of being attacked and punished can be avoided. If this happens, the person can also become his or her own Higher Power.

Our relationship to our father influences our ideas about the Higher Power. This fact is hardly ever conscious, and even religious professionals often don't realize that although their theology is impeccable, their actual *trust level* regarding their Higher Power is very low because of long-forgotten abuse issues.

A person's first experience of a Higher Power in this culture is his or her experience with Dad (sometimes Mom, but mainly Dad). The way Dad treated you becomes at some level how you think a Higher Power is going to treat you.

- If Dad abandoned you, you become your own Higher Power, believing that you can accomplish your own recovery. You have difficulty believing in a Higher Power outside yourself.

- If Dad enmeshed with you and used you for his own needs (to take care of him or his responsibilities in the family), you also may become your own Higher Power and be unable to believe a Higher Power exists outside yourself.

- If Dad neglected you, you may believe a Higher Power exists, but you may not think a Higher Power will help you or restore you to sanity.

- If Dad attacked you, you may believe a Higher Power exists and might restore you to sanity, but the process will be painful and shaming because you think of a Higher Power as harsh and punishing.

WHAT TO DO

Review what you wrote about your history of abuse from your father in part 1 of the workbook. Describe here how your father treated you: abandonment, enmeshment, ignoring, or attacking. (It is possible to have been treated with a blend of two or more of these.) Then write about how this has affected the way you relate to a Higher Power. (In some family systems, the mother has more power than the father and is seen as the highest power in the family by the child. If that was the case in your childhood, write about your relationship to your mother.)

EXAMPLE

My father ignored me when I was doing things he approved of, but he was very critical and harsh when I did something he didn't like. So I had a blend: both being attacked and also ignored.

The effect on my relationship to a Higher Power is that I fear an attack from my Higher Power when I am less than perfect. I also feel that in any other circumstance, my Higher Power is not there for me or is ignoring me. I never really have been my own Higher Power even though my mother enmeshed with me and I took care of her. But in terms of power within the family, my mother was so diminished by my father that he's the main concept of a Higher Power that I have.

How My Father Treated Me in Childhood:

How This Affected My View of the Way a Higher Power Would Relate to Me:

Now that you have examined the relationship between your father's treatment of you and your beliefs about the Higher Power, write what you are coming to believe is a more accurate picture of the Higher Power as a caring, healing power both greater than yourself and greater than your parents.

There are many ways to envision a Higher Power who can lovingly restore you to sanity in a positive, respectful way. For example, one person might envision this power through the Christian tradition as a trinity made up of God the Creator, Jesus Christ, and the Holy Spirit; while another person might have a visual image of a bright white light that is feminine in nature. Each person's concept of a Higher Power is very personal. We did not provide a specific example for this because we felt that to do so might limit your own freedom to express your beliefs about this vital concept.

How I Envision My Higher Power (greater than myself, greater than my parents)

Consider the definition of *sanity* to be the ability to look at ourselves as "perfectly imperfect" without experiencing inordinate amounts of pain, fear, anger, guilt, or shame that can make us feel crazy. We are sane when we can know that being imperfect is normal. Now describe a time when you noted yourself being normally (perfectly) imperfect and experienced overwhelming feelings about it, thinking something was wrong with you. Describe both the situation and the feelings.

EXAMPLE

I realized several hours after it happened that I had gossiped about my husband and criticized him. I felt intense shame, guilt, pain, and fear, and wanted to disappear in my room and cry.

Times I Have Noticed Myself Being "Perfectly Imperfect" and Had Overwhelming Feelings

Step Three

> *"Made a decision to turn our will and our lives over to the care of God as we understood God."*

PURPOSE OF EXERCISE

This step is an act of faith that a loving, life-changing Higher Power will be there for you as you turn your life over to its care. The purpose of these exercises is to help you see more clearly how you live life according to your own will rather than turning your will and your life over to a Higher Power.

BACKGROUND READING

The following paragraphs are the background reading assignment for this step.

We are responsible for acting in our own best interest in our lives, making sure that we are taking care of ourselves without offending other people in that process. It is our responsibility to make an effort at change. We work at changing regardless of a Higher Power. When we reach the point where we can see that using our will is not enough to make a change take place, we can use Step Three. When we are in a state of powerlessness and become aware that we can't change any further, we then turn our will over to our Higher Power to assist us in changing, and we let go of determining how we're going to change or even *if* we're going to change. This is a "letting-go" step.

I usually say something like, "Okay, Higher Power, I've done all I can. I can't do the changing that I know I need to do. Therefore, I turn myself over to your will for me. If I change it will be because it is your will. If I don't change, I will live in that experience and learn to embrace myself in my perfect imperfection, which is also your will for me."

I believe that this step is third in the order of steps because if we truly do Step One and become aware of our disease, we have a tendency to feel overwhelmed with how "sick" we are. In Step Two, we see that our behavior is self-defeating to the point of insanity. At this point, Step Three keeps us from being overwhelmed by what we learned in Steps One and Two. We say, in effect, "Higher Power, I turn my skewed reality and my codependent life over to you to deal with. I can hardly stand to even acknowledge my codependence right now."

But even though this step is a beginning to "let go and let a Higher Power," at this stage of recovery we are not as able to turn our will and our lives over to the care of a Higher Power as we will be after working the rest of the steps. We will gain a lot more information as we look at how our disease has impacted the lives of others with whom we are in relationship, and then we'll know more specifically what we have to turn over.

As pointed out by two Alcoholics Anonymous speakers (Joe and Charlie), the first three words of the step –"Made a decision"– are very important. At this stage of recovery, most of us really don't know how to turn our will and our lives over to the care of a Higher Power. But we *make a decision* that our intention is to do just that. And in the process of working Steps Four through Twelve, the Higher Power will teach us how to let go, how to stop solving everything ourselves, how to stop using our own will, how to stop trying to control the outcome of our lives. The decision is "Yes, I'm going to learn how to turn it over and I'm going to begin learning by doing the next step and then the next one until I've done all twelve."

What To Do

Begin to notice yourself struggling to use your own will, make a change by yourself, solve a problem alone, control the outcome of your life or someone else's, but then remember to use Step Three and turn it over to a Higher Power. Whenever this happens, describe here the issue, the process you went through to arrive at Step Three, what happened with regard to the situation after you released it, and how you felt emotionally before and after turning it over.

EXAMPLE

DATE: July 1988   Situation (Problem, Change, Etc.):

My cousin is engaged to be married. I have met her fiancée and I can see that they will never get along over the years. I keep going over in my mind how to tell them so I can help them avoid a tragic mistake.

How I Realized I Must Turn It Over:

I discussed the problem with my sponsor. She asked me, "If someone had told you not to marry your first husband, would that have stopped you?" I realized someone DID try to tell me that we weren't compatible, but I was sure I could see something they couldn't and I knew they were wrong. I married him and we were soon divorced. I was wrong, but I hadn't been able to hear any of the people who'd tried to tell me. To find some inner peace about my cousin's engagement, I realized I needed to acknowledge that ultimately a Higher Power is in charge of things, not me, and that includes my cousin's marriage. So I turned my life and my will and my cousin's marriage in particular over to my Higher Power.

What Happened After I Released It:

Several months later, my cousin and her fiancée broke up. My cousin told me that she and this man had worked on problem areas between them for months and he just couldn't feel comfortable marrying her, so he broke it off. She was very hurt. For eight months she grieved. But then she met a great guy who is much more like her and they are happily dating.

How I Felt

Before:

Fearful and anxious

After:

Calm, serene

Times When I Have Turned Situations Over to a Higher Power

1. DATE:

   Situation (Problem, Change, Etc.):

How I Realized I Must Turn It Over:

What Happened After I Released It:

How I Felt Before:

After:

2. DATE:

Situation (Problem, Change, Etc.):

How I Realized I Must Turn It Over:

What Happened After I Released It:

How I Felt Before: **After:**

What Happened After I Released It:

How I Felt Before: **After:**

What Happened After I Released It:

How I Felt Before: **After:**

What Happened After I Released It:

How I Felt Before: **After:**

What Happened After I Released It:

How I Felt Before: **After:**

Sometimes you turn certain issues over to a Higher Power and then you resume using your own will in the situation, or take it back from the Higher Power. Write here about any situation you have written about earlier that you have taken back, each time you take it back. Note the dates to see whether you are letting progressively more time pass before you take a problem back.

EXAMPLE

DATE: Oct. 1988   **Situation:**

My cousin's engagement: almost told her I thought they were incompatible and was glad the guy had broken up with her.

DATE: Oct. 1988   **What Made Me Re-turn It Over:**

Saw her pain and decided my comment was unnecessary and might hurt her relationship with me. Put it back in the Higher Power's control.

Times When I Have Re-turned Situations Over

1. **DATE:**

   Situation:

DATE:

What Made Me Re-turn It Over:

2. DATE:

Situation:

DATE:

What Made Me Re-turn It Over:

3. DATE:

Situation:

DATE:

What Made Me Re-turn It Over:

4. DATE:

Situation:

DATE:

What Made Me Re-turn It Over:

Step Four

> ## *"Made a searching and fearless moral inventory of ourselves."*

PURPOSE OF EXERCISE

Even though your parents are responsible and accountable for what happened to you in childhood, you are now in charge of your life and your recovery. You alone can work to become nonoffensive in your relationships. This step is designed to help you see how you are being offensive as an adult so that you can change and heal through working Steps Seven through Twelve.

Step Four is a moral inventory. For the codependent specifically, it is a look at how you have authentically offended other people. "Authentic offense" means that by your behavior you have been disrespectful of someone else's boundary. For example, screaming at someone because you are angry is an act of verbal offense. Hugging or touching someone who does not wish to be touched or without his or her permission is an act of physical offense. Relying on a child to meet your need for emotional intimacy instead of being there to meet the child's need and relying on your spouse or a significant adult for emotional intimacy is an act of emotional sexual offense toward that child.

Authentic offense does not include situations in which someone notices what you look like or what you are thinking, feeling, or doing, and doesn't like it. That person may have feelings and thoughts about what he or she has noticed and tell you that he or she is offended. But your appearance, thinking, feelings, and behavior are not acts of authentic offense if you have not disregarded anyone's boundaries.

For example, a husband may feel angry and hurt on Father's Day because his wife did not contact all the grown children to arrange a family backyard barbecue for him. He may express his anger and hurt at his wife for her "neglect." But she may think that it is not her job to make Father's Day happen for her husband—it is the job of his children. So she has not authentically offended him by this "neglect." Therefore, she has not committed an act of authentic offense even though her husband perceives that her neglect has caused his anger and pain. He is simply in a codependent state of blaming other people for what he is thinking and feeling. She uses her internal boundary to be present and listen to his thoughts and feelings, noting the impact of her behavior, having feelings about seeing a loved one in distress, but not *taking responsibility* for his distress.

Before you write about your disregard of the boundaries of others, I will ask you to review the corresponding chapter in *Facing Codependence*, as well as your writing in Step One about the condition of each area of your boundary system. This is because where you have damaged boundaries or none at all, you are likely to be offensive to others in that same area.

Here are the ground rules for the following exercises:

1. As you do the background reading to review the various kinds of abuse, look this time for ways in which you have been the offender, not the victim.

2. Limit the time span of your inventory to *your* adult life—the time period from age eighteen to the present. The reason for this is that when you were a child and were committing abusive or offensive acts toward anyone, you did this because your boundaries weren't fully developed and also because *no adult caretaker was confronting your offensive behavior, correcting and guiding you* to adjust your thinking, feelings, and behavior toward being nonoffensive. Or your caregiver(s) set you up by giving you a responsibility that was over your head and that you *could not handle in a functional way* because you were a child and not an adult. In my opinion, these instances do not belong in a Step Four inventory.

3. Look at how you have offended both adults and children.

4. Examine your attitudes and judgments as well as your actions. Step Four is not only about your behavior, but also about offensive *attitudes and judgments*. It is important that you be as thorough and specific as possible in the following writing since this material will be the basis for later steps.

PHYSICAL OFFENSES

BACKGROUND READING

Chapter 10 of *Facing Codependence*, and your writing in Step One of this workbook about the condition of your external-physical boundary.

Anything that violates another person's right to control how, when, where, and by whom his or her body is touched is considered to be an authentic act of physical offense. Here is a review of your physical rights:

1. As an adult, nobody has the right to touch you without your permission. Also, you do not have the right to touch anyone without that person's permission.

2. People to whom you have given permission to touch you may touch you only in the way in which you want to be touched. Also, if someone gives you permission to touch him or her, you only may touch the person in the way in which that person wants to be touched.

3. It's your responsibility to take control of how, when, where, and who touches you. You need to be able to exercise that control with most people, unless you're dealing with a major offender. Also, in recovery, you need to be able to respect the rights of others over how, when, where, and who touches them. You do not "give" them the right; it is already the right of everyone. Rather, you learn to recognize it and respect it.

WHAT TO DO

Review your relationships with adults (age eighteen and up) in your life, including those with your spouse or former spouse(s), parents (after you were eighteen), siblings (after they were eighteen), adult children, co-workers, friends, acquaintances, and strangers. Use the following space to describe instances when you have disregarded the physical boundary of any adult.

EXAMPLE

NAME: Aunt Bett   **DATE:** Since 10/82

WHAT HAPPENED: Whenever I go see Aunt Bett in the nursing home I give her a hearty hug. She always cringes and withdraws, but I ignore it. I hug her so the nurses and anyone else who is watching won't think I don't like Aunt Bett. Perhaps with her severe arthritis I have been hurting her. I have not gotten her permission to hug her and have ignored her physical indications.

How I Have Disregarded Physical Boundaries of Adults

NAME: **DATE:**
WHAT HAPPENED:

NAME: **DATE:**
WHAT HAPPENED:

NAME: **DATE:**
WHAT HAPPENED:

NAME: **DATE:**
WHAT HAPPENED:

NAME: **DATE:**

WHAT HAPPENED:

NAME: **DATE:**

WHAT HAPPENED:

Now review your relationships with children (age seventeen and under), including your own children and any other children with whom you have come into contact (in the classroom, baby-sitting, at the church nursery, at swimming lessons, coaching, in scout troops, as guests in your home, and so on. In the following space, describe instances when you have disregarded the physical boundary of any child.

EXAMPLE

NAME: Jimmy   **DATE:** Last week
WHAT HAPPENED: I sat down next to Jimmy on the couch to watch ''Sesame Street'' with him. He squirmed and said, ''Mom, would you move over? I feel squashed.'' I laughed at him and said, ''No, Jimmy. I like to sit this close to you. It feels good.'' I made him sit there and violated his need for space.

How I Have Disregarded Physical Boundaries of Children

NAME: **DATE:**
WHAT HAPPENED:

NAME: **DATE:**
WHAT HAPPENED:

NAME: **DATE:**

WHAT HAPPENED:

NAME: **DATE:**

WHAT HAPPENED:

NAME: **DATE:**

WHAT HAPPENED:

NAME: **DATE:**

WHAT HAPPENED:

SEXUAL OFFENSES

BACKGROUND READING

Chapter 11 of *Facing Codependence*, and your writing in Step One of this workbook about the condition of your external-sexual boundary.

Each person has the right to determine with whom, where, when, and how he or she will be sexual. Any healthy sexual activity you engage in with another adult is done with that person's full consent and agreement and does not violate commitments you have made to another person. (For example, a commitment to be faithful to a wife or husband would mean that having a sexual relationship with another person would fall into the category of authentic sexual abuse to your permanent partner and possibly to the outside person you are having sex with and her or his partner.) And where children are concerned, no adult should ever do anything sexual with a child, no matter what behavior the child may be doing that may lead an adult to think the child "wants" to be sexual.

WHAT TO DO

Review your relationships with adults in your life, and use the following space to describe instances when you have disregarded the sexual boundary of any adult.

EXAMPLE

NAME: Sherrie (my wife)　　　**DATE:** all the time
WHAT HAPPENED: I insist that my wife have sex with me every night, even when she is too tired or uncomfortable from her monthly cycle. Sometimes she tries to decline, but I know how to act cute and cuddly and pester her until she finally gives in. I realize she probably decides it's less trouble to "get it over with" than argue with me endlessly about it.

How I Have Disregarded Sexual Boundaries of Adults

NAME: DATE:

WHAT HAPPENED:

NAME: DATE:

WHAT HAPPENED:

NAME: **DATE:**

WHAT HAPPENED:

NAME: **DATE:**

WHAT HAPPENED:

NAME: **DATE:**

WHAT HAPPENED:

NAME: **DATE:**

WHAT HAPPENED:

Now review your relationships with children in your life, and use the following space to describe instances when you have disregarded the sexual boundary of any child.

EXAMPLE

NAME: Cindi   **DATE:** last week

WHAT HAPPENED: I came into my 12-year-old daughter's room when she had just started getting dressed. She jumped, jerked her gown in front of her, and said, "Daddy, don't you ever knock!?" I got angry and said, "Don't be ridiculous, I'm your father. I don't have to knock." I was insensitive to her right to privacy and embarrassed her sexually. I also put myself above the rule of knocking before entering anyone's private space.

NAME: Sally   **DATE:** 10/76

WHAT HAPPENED: My daughter had a slumber party for her 16th birthday. The next morning I made comments to her that she had the best-looking boobs of all her friends. She blushed and looked miserable, but I kept on kidding her about how she and the other girls looked in their nightgowns.

How I Have Disregarded Sexual Boundaries of Children

NAME: **DATE:**
WHAT HAPPENED:

NAME: **DATE:**
WHAT HAPPENED:

NAME: **DATE:**

WHAT HAPPENED:

NAME: **DATE:**

WHAT HAPPENED:

NAME: **DATE:**

WHAT HAPPENED:

NAME: **DATE:**

WHAT HAPPENED:

EMOTIONAL OFFENSES

<table>
<tr>
<td>

**BACKGROUND
READING**

</td>
<td>

Chapter 12 of *Facing Codependence*, and your writing in Step One of this workbook about the condition of your internal-emotional boundary.

You commit an authentic act of emotional abuse whenever you violate anyone's internal boundary by manipulating or attempting to control his or her feelings.

</td>
</tr>
<tr>
<td>

WHAT TO DO

</td>
<td>

Review your relationships with adults in your life, and use the following space to describe instances when you have disregarded the internal-emotional boundary of any adult.

</td>
</tr>
</table>

EXAMPLE

> **NAME:** Sandy **DATE:** 10/87
> **WHAT HAPPENED:** My girlfriend told me she was hurt because I hadn't called her for a week. I told her she didn't feel hurt, she felt jealous and possessive and I couldn't stand a possessive woman. I did not accept her word that she was hurt.

How I Have Disregarded Internal-Emotional Boundaries of Adults

NAME: **DATE:**

WHAT HAPPENED:

NAME: **DATE:**

WHAT HAPPENED:

NAME: **DATE:**
WHAT HAPPENED:

NAME: **DATE:**
WHAT HAPPENED:

NAME: **DATE:**

WHAT HAPPENED:

NAME: **DATE:**

WHAT HAPPENED:

Now review your relationships with children in your life, and use the following space to describe instances when you have disregarded the internal-emotional boundary of any child.

EXAMPLE

NAME: Brenda   **DATE:** 9/88
WHAT HAPPENED: I baby-sat with my 3-year-old niece. When she cried and asked for her mommy, I told her she didn't really feel sad, she was just hungry, and I got her some cookies and milk. I wouldn't talk to her about her sadness, and since she quit crying as she ate the cookies, I thought I had solved the problem.

How I Have Disregarded Internal-Emotional Boundaries of Children

NAME: **DATE:**

WHAT HAPPENED:

NAME: **DATE:**

WHAT HAPPENED:

NAME: **DATE:**
WHAT HAPPENED:

NAME: **DATE:**
WHAT HAPPENED:

NAME: **DATE:**
WHAT HAPPENED:

NAME: **DATE:**
WHAT HAPPENED:

INTELLECTUAL OFFENSES

BACKGROUND READING

Chapter 13 of *Facing Codependence,* and your writing in Step One of this workbook about the condition of your internal-intellectual boundary.

All people have the right to think what they think. They only need to face the consequences of their thinking. Yet in your disease of codependence, you are likely to interfere with the right of other people to have their thinking and the consequences of it. If you are actively in your disease of codependence and disregarding people's internal thinking boundary, you try to reason, argue, and/or demand that they change their thinking for your own comfort, in a misguided attempt to help them avoid the consequences you think they are going to have by thinking the way they do. Or perhaps your motivation is that their thinking about YOU is not to your liking and you can't stand to have people thinking that way about you.

In recovery, with good internal boundaries, you will be able to have inner peace even when someone else has the "wrong idea" about you. A useful phrase I have heard for times like these is "Just because he/she thinks that doesn't make it true for me."

With children, who need your guidance, it is likely that you have authentically offended them by giving your guidance in a shaming, authoritarian way.

WHAT TO DO

Review your relationships with adults in your life, and use the following chart to describe instances when you have disregarded the internal-intellectual boundary of any adult.

EXAMPLE

NAME: Tim   **DATE:** 2/81
WHAT HAPPENED: I told my boyfriend Tim that he didn't want to go to Yale because the students were stuck-up, but that he wanted to go to Texas Tech where everyone was friendlier. In reality, I wanted him to be nearer to me while I finished high school. He did go to Texas Tech, but we broke up a year later. He could have done very well at Yale . . . he was very smart.

How I Have Disregarded Internal-Intellectual Boundaries of Adults

NAME: **DATE:**

WHAT HAPPENED:

NAME: **DATE:**

WHAT HAPPENED:

NAME: **DATE:**

WHAT HAPPENED:

NAME: **DATE:**

WHAT HAPPENED:

NAME: **DATE:**
WHAT HAPPENED:

NAME: **DATE:**
WHAT HAPPENED:

Now review your relationships with children in your life, and use the following space to describe instances when you have disregarded the internal-intellectual boundary of any child.

EXAMPLE

NAME: Bobby   **DATE:** July
WHAT HAPPENED: My 14-year-old son wanted to try out for football at school. I told him he didn't want to do that, but should try out on his drums for the band. I controlled his reality about football because I was afraid he would get hurt playing the game.

How I Have Disregarded Internal-Intellectual Boundaries of Children

NAME: **DATE:**

WHAT HAPPENED:

NAME: **DATE:**

WHAT HAPPENED:

NAME: **DATE:**

WHAT HAPPENED:

NAME: **DATE:**

WHAT HAPPENED:

NAME: **DATE:**

WHAT HAPPENED:

NAME: **DATE:**

WHAT HAPPENED:

SPIRITUAL OFFENSES

BACKGROUND READING

Chapter 14 of *Facing Codependence*, and your writing in Step One of this workbook about the condition of your internal-spiritual boundary.

To live a mature life as a recovering adult, you must be able to have a positive relationship to a power that is truly greater than you are.

You engage in authentic spiritual abuse whenever you demand to be someone else's Higher Power. This is most often done when you give yourself the right to determine what someone else will look like, think, feel, or do or not do.

It is also spiritually abusive to insist that someone else be your Higher Power. While it is true that the Higher Power can communicate with you through people, you must be aware that a human being is only a channel, not the Higher Power. Your understanding of such a Higher Power may be limited at first, but through working the steps it will mature. Relying on a human being to be your Higher Power leads only to disappointment, frustration, and brokenness in the relationship, whether the person is a parent, a spouse, a sponsor in the program, a minister, a therapist, an author of a helpful book, or a friend. The Higher Power is not another human being, and putting a human being in that position in your life is an act of spiritual abuse toward that person.

It is also an act of spiritual offense to give a person the message that there is something wrong with him or her. There is a healthy and functional way to express yourself (thoughts, feelings, behaviors) to other people that doesn't diminish, demean, belittle, accuse, or shame the other person. You say simply, "This is what you did [said, or whatever] and this is how I feel about it [hurt, frightened, angry]." This approach doesn't analyze, judge, criticize, call names, or condemn. When you analyze, judge, criticize, or condemn someone, you are spiritually offending the other person by attacking the fact that he or she is a precious, fallible human being (who may have the disease of codependence or not, is not perfect, and is likely to be offensive at times).

If you are a parent, it is necessary and appropriate for you to act as a Higher Power toward your children for a while. Since the child's concept of a Higher Power comes from you, it is your responsibility to model a nurturing, affirming, and appropriately structuring Higher Power, so that the child's concept of a Higher Power is functional. But when you parent in the way that humiliates or shames the child inordinately, then you are spiritually offending that child.

Functional parenting leads a child to a relationship with a Higher Power that is greater than the child and greater than you are. You do not cover up your own fallibility in dealing with your child. You admit it and face it. It is an authentic act of spiritual offense to offend a child (or anyone) and then refuse to offer amends and to make restitution. When you are wrong in some way in the relationship with your child (or anyone), or are imperfect in a way that the child can observe, you admit it, make amends, and make restitution where necessary. This can be done without losing your position of authority or the respect and love of your child. Hiding your imperfections from your child is an act of authentic spiritual abuse toward that child (unless it involves an area of your life that is none of the child's business). The message the child gets from a "perfect parent" is that when the child grows up, he or she will never fail either, which is far from reality, or that he or she was not valuable enough to deserve apologies and amends.

WHAT TO DO

Review your relationships with adults in your life, and use the following space to describe instances when you have disregarded the spiritual boundary of any adult.

EXAMPLE

NAME: Janice   **DATE:** Last week
WHAT HAPPENED: My best friend has helped me through every crisis I have had since we met 10 years ago. I cannot make a decision without asking her opinion first. In fact, I usually wind up doing what she says. Lately, she's been getting vague about her answers to my problems. I got really mad last time and told her she was letting me down. I have been insisting that she be my Higher Power.

How I Have Disregarded Spiritual Boundaries of Adults

NAME: **DATE:**

WHAT HAPPENED:

NAME: **DATE:**

WHAT HAPPENED:

NAME: **DATE:**

WHAT HAPPENED:

NAME: **DATE:**

WHAT HAPPENED:

NAME: **DATE:**

WHAT HAPPENED:

NAME: **DATE:**

WHAT HAPPENED:

Now review your relationships with children in your life, and use the following space to describe instances when you have disregarded the spiritual boundary of any child.

EXAMPLE

NAME: Matt   **DATE:** 11/88

WHAT HAPPENED: My 10-year-old son asked me why he had to go to bed at 8:00 every night when other kids in his class stayed up until 9:00. I told him that he had to do what I said as long as he lived in this house and that he'd better not *ever* question our household rules. I didn't give him the right to have his own thoughts but taught him I was the god of the family and would do all the thinking.

How I Have Disregarded Spiritual Boundaries of Children

NAME: **DATE:**

WHAT HAPPENED:

NAME: **DATE:**

WHAT HAPPENED:

NAME: **DATE:**

WHAT HAPPENED:

NAME: **DATE:**

WHAT HAPPENED:

NAME: **DATE:**

WHAT HAPPENED:

NAME: **DATE:**

WHAT HAPPENED:

Step Five

"*Admitted to God, to ourselves, and to another human being the exact nature of our wrongs.*"

Now that you have written as much as you can about the various forms of authentic offense and how you have disregarded the boundaries of those with whom you are in relationship, Step Five is necessary to keep moving into recovery.

BACKGROUND READING

Read the following paragraphs before doing this exercise.

ADMITTED TO GOD, TO OURSELVES . . .

As you approach and while you are doing Step Five, try to keep God as you understand God in your consciousness—a caring, nonjudgmental power greater than you, your parents, and the person who is listening to your admission.

As you tell another person the exact nature of your wrongs, I believe it is important also to be especially aware yourself of what you are saying. The process is more like admitting to ourselves and God (whom we are keeping in our consciousness) while the other person is just there listening. In other words, doing Step Five is more than quickly reading off your lists of offenses toward others from your workbook without really hearing yourself.

. . . AND TO ANOTHER HUMAN BEING . . .

Describing the characteristics of someone who would be a good person to do your Step Five with is difficult. If I made a list of ideal characteristics, no one could measure up because no perfect human beings exist. But here are a few guidelines. I think it is important for the person hearing your Step Five to be

- someone whom you trust to keep this information confidential

- someone who is the same sex as you, unless you are homosexual

- someone who has done this step himself or herself and is in a Twelve-Step program for his or her own codependence

- someone who has a sense of a power greater than himself or herself and greater than the person's own parents, and whose Higher Power is not another human being (sponsor, therapist, or whomever)

- someone who is, in your mind, clearly not your Higher Power

- someone who does not demand to be your Higher Power by attempting to create your reality for you (telling you what you should feel or think or do). Instead, this person needs to have the capacity to be with you as you share your thoughts and feelings and let you have them without trying to interrupt, change anything, or interfere in any way. This person just supports you by listening and letting you be right where you are.

. . . THE EXACT NATURE OF OUR WRONGS

"The exact nature of our wrongs" is how we've offended other people's boundaries. You've described the exact nature of your wrongs in the lists you have written for Step Four about your disregarding the boundaries of adults and children in your life. You say out loud in the presence of another human being: "This is what I did to violate someone else's boundaries." You may wish to take this workbook with you and use it as a guideline as you explain exactly what happened between you and these other people.

As you do this step, talk about what happened, and every time you notice an emotion, no matter what you are saying at the moment, stop to name the emotion and allow yourself to experience the feelings. You might simply say, "I'm feeling really sad about this" (or whatever the emotion is).

WHAT TO DO

1. Choose someone to whom you will tell how you have disregarded other people's boundaries. Ask that person to hear your Step Five. If that person is not free to do so at this time, choose someone else and ask that person. When you find someone who can hear your Step Five, write that person's name here:

_____

2. Make an appointment with him or her. Write the time and date of the appointment here:

_____

3. After you have met with this person and told him or her your Step Five, use the following space to reflect about what it was like. You may choose to include such things as a general description of what was said, how you felt before you started, how you felt during the step itself, and how you felt afterward. If you identified any general patterns about yourself in this process, note them here.

Reflections on My Experience with Step Five

Step Six

PURPOSE OF EXERCISE

The purposes of Step Six are (1) to identify the defects of character you are now ready to see, having done Steps Four and Five, and (2) to become willing to live without them and learn a more mature way to live.

By doing Steps Four and Five you began to see yourself as having problems. These problems are defects of character that come out of your experiences of powerlessness and the unmanageable consequences of the core symptoms. Codependent character defects are attitudes, feelings, and behaviors you hang on to that sabotage your happiness and relationships and keep you from taking responsibility for your own life and recovery. Once you have recognized these character defects, you can then make a decision that you are ready to have the Higher Power remove them.

Recognizing how these character defects are sabotaging your life by affecting you and also the people in relationship with you is a painful process. It has been said that recovery is a pain-driven process. Until you get into enough pain, you are not motivated to do anything about genuine recovery.

BACKGROUND READING

Following are descriptions of several typical character defects many codependents have, along with a discussion of how each defect sabotages your life when you try to relate to others using these shortcomings. We have not attempted to list every possible character defect, nor do we mean to say that each codependent has them all. Use this selection as a beginning place from which to draw up your personal list of character defects. Read each description, then do the writing exercise for any that apply to you before proceeding to the next one.

PEOPLE-PLEASING

People-pleasing is dishonest, can provoke unnecessary arguments, and can produce resentment toward others. Here's a brief description of each of these three sabotaging effects.

DISHONESTY

You give up what you really want and do what someone else wants, because your doing so pleases that person. You avoid saying what you mean because you believe saying something else would please that person more. You make commitments to people for things you do not want to do or cannot do without a lot of trouble — even things you don't know how to do, so that you have to go through a learning process before you can accomplish the thing you have agreed to do.

You deceive the other person into thinking (1) that you like to do these things because you commit to do them, (2) that the things you say represent your true feelings, your true self, and (3) that you do and say these things because they enhance your own life and make you happy in and of themselves.

How this sabotages your life: The other person cannot relate to the real person you are, because you have hidden yourself from him or her.

UNNECESSARY ARGUMENTS

When you are people-pleasing, you are embroiled in commitments and activities that do not enhance your life or bring you joy. But you tell yourself you are willing to do them to please the other person, and that person's pleasure enhances your life. The problem with this is, if the person doesn't exhibit the pleasure you think he or she should or doesn't express gratitude for your participation in the activity, your life is not enhanced and you feel anger, fear, or pain. The purpose of putting yourself through these undesirable behaviors and commitments has backfired, and instead of enhancement you feel diminished by your anger, fear, and/or pain.

In your codependence, you are very likely to hold the other person responsible for your diminishment. Since you deceived the other person into thinking you *chose* these commitments and behaviors, expressing your anger directly sounds bizarre to the other person. The other person's response is something like, "But I thought you *wanted* to eat at this restaurant." "I thought you *preferred* to go alone to pick up the children at camp." Your deception causes an automatic deadlock in the communication.

How this sabotages your life: The other person is deceived, baffled, defensive. You have subjected that person to unnecessary arguments and attacks growing out of your misdirected anger at the person for things he or she has no awareness of.

RESENTMENT

When you engage in people-pleasing, you often assume that a nonspoken agreement exists between you and the other person and that he or she will treat you in a similar people-pleasing manner. After you've given up what you want to do in favor of pleasing the other person, a time comes when you expect the same "courtesy" from the other person. When the person, who has no idea that this nonspoken agreement is in your mind, does not reciprocate, resentment builds and you subject the other person to your "retaliation," whether it be aggressive and outright anger or passive retaliation on a more subtle level.

I'm not talking about when you make a clear choice to compromise and, for example, go with the other person to a certain movie, as long as the reason for your choice is clear to the other person. For example, a choice between seeing one of two movies, a comedy and a spy mystery, comes up. You might prefer the spy mystery while the other person really enjoys comedies more. If you can say, "Comedies are not my favorite kind of movie, but I'll go with you because you want to see it and because I want to be with you. Next time we go to a movie I'd like to go to the spy mystery and would enjoy having you go with me," that is a clear communication. Even if the other person does not ever want to go to the spy mystery, he or she isn't deceived into thinking you preferred the comedy.

The situation becomes people-pleasing when you pretend to *prefer* the comedy and withhold from the other person the honest reason you are going to the comedy. Then, later, when you bring up the spy mystery movie and the other person's response is lukewarm or negative, resentment pops up. You think, "That's not fair! I cheerfully went to the comedy with him (her) and now it's his (her) turn. He (She) never does things I want to do." You turn sour and sullen, distancing yourself, and the other person has no idea what is going on with you.

How this sabotages your life: The other person is subjected to your unexpected "retaliation" methods when your resentment comes up about something he or she did not have information about.

WHAT TO DO

Use the following space to describe how people-pleasing operates in your life, if it does. Use these questions as a guideline for writing about it:

1. How does people-pleasing harm you and keep you from being in recovery?

2. How does it affect others adversely and block intimacy?

3. Are you ready to have the Higher Power remove this defect and learn to live without it?

4. If not, what are you gaining by holding on to it?

How People-Pleasing Operates in My Life

1. How does people-pleasing harm you and keep you from being in recovery?

2. How does if affect others adversely and block intimacy?

3. Are you ready to have the Higher Power remove this defect and learn to live without it?

4. If not, what are you gaining by holding on to it?

PERFECTIONISM

Perfectionism is that compulsive drive to do things perfectly, leaving no detail imperfect. Since no one can perform this way all the time in the real world, perfectionism leads to dishonest cover-ups, and when a cover-up is impossible, unnecessary pain and agony result when your mistakes are revealed. You also can shut others out of your life with perfectionism. Here's a brief description of how each of these sabotaging processes operates.

DISHONEST COVER-UPS

Since making a mistake is so painful, you often construct massive cover-ups to prevent others from knowing about your mistakes. If you are confronted with a mistake, but engage in long explanations and justifications about why your error wasn't really an error, or how it was somebody else's fault, you are engaging in such a cover-up.

How this sabotages your life: Living with a person who never seems to make a mistake or cannot admit it when the mistake comes to light, is painful for other people in relationship with you. When one person *is* able to admit making mistakes, even though you respond with kind, benevolent forgiveness, the fact that you don't seem to err makes the honest person's mistakes even more painful to confess. And as your children watch you with the innocent eyes that only children have, they see your mistakes and the way you cover them up and learn to model their behavior after yours and cover up their own mistakes. Or if they buy into your "perfection," they may become intensely intimidated by you and shamed by their own natural imperfections.

UNNECESSARY PAIN AND EMBARRASSMENT

Sometimes it is inevitable that your mistakes will catch up to you and be known by others and yourself, with no way to hide them and no one to blame them on. Reacting to such mistakes with painful agony, crying, and/or anger implies that you think you should have been perfect and not made any mistake.

How this sabotages your life: With this attitude toward mistakes, you are subjecting the people in your life to unnecessary anguish, since they must deal with you while you have your (unnecessary and inappropriate) pain and anger.

SHUTTING OUT OTHERS

Becoming absorbed in a task to the degree it takes to do it "perfectly" is very likely to remove you physically and emotionally from the other people in your life. It takes more time, your level of concentration is very deep, and you are not as emotionally available to others as you could be if you could lighten up. As I have learned from my husband, Pat, "some things are worth doing, but worth doing poorly." That translates to me in certain circumstances, "Go on and get it over with and move on with life and relationships that are more important than how I did some routine task perfectly or prepared for an informal party in my home as if it were a wedding reception for the governor and his wife."

How this sabotages your life: Other people may often feel shut out, afraid to interrupt you even with a legitimate need or just because they want to spend time with you. You may often be telling friends, "Not now, I'm busy," when you are busy with myriad details of perfecting something that doesn't matter as much as healthy relationships matter. Perfectionism can be used as a wall of protection from relationships in which you are uncomfortable because of the pain of being in the less-than position.

WHAT TO DO

Use the following space to describe how perfectionism operates in your life, if it does. Use these questions as a guideline for writing about it:

1. How does trying to do everything "perfectly" harm you and keep you from being in recovery?

2. How does it affect others adversely and block intimacy?

3. Are you ready to have the Higher Power remove your perfectionism and learn to live without it?

4. If not, what are you gaining by holding on to it?

How Perfectionism Operates in My Life

1. How does trying to do everything "perfectly" harm you and keep you from being in recovery?

2. How does it affect others adversely and block intimacy?

3. Are you ready to have the Higher Power remove your perfectionism and learn to live without it?

4. If not, what are you gaining by holding on to it?

STRIVING FOR POWER

When you approach life from the better-than position, you are often in power struggles with those with whom you relate. In a power struggle, each of the combatants is struggling for the right to be in charge of what the other one does, when it is done, who is right, what the rules are, when they can be broken, and so on. This striving may take place at home with your mate and children, at work with your boss or subordinates, or socially with friends. Whether you win or lose the struggle, the other person is affected just by your engaging in such struggles in the first place.

How this sabotages your life: Relating to a person who continually tries to be in power is very difficult. If you are the power-hungry person and win a power struggle, the other person usually winds up in the less-than position, which does not feel good. Thus, staying in a relationship with you requires that the other person be willing to tolerate this less-than position.

Whether you win or not, the fact that you treat relationships as a power struggle and constantly attempt to win means that the other people around you must often put out energy and effort to defend against you in the struggle for power, which can be exhausting and discouraging.

WHAT TO DO

Use the following space to describe how striving for power operates in your life, if it does. Use these questions as a guideline for writing about it:

1. How does always having to be right, in control, or having the last word harm you and keep you from being in recovery?

2. How does striving for power affect others adversely and block intimacy?

3. Are you ready to have the Higher Power remove your power hunger and learn to live without it?

4. If not, what are you gaining by holding on to your need to "win" in your relationships?

How Striving for Power Operates in My Life

1. How does always having to be right, in control, or having the last word harm you and keep you from being in recovery?

2. How does striving for power affect others adversely and block intimacy?

3. Are you ready to have the Higher Power remove your power hunger and learn to live without it?

4. If not, what are you gaining by holding on to your need to "win" in your relationships?

OVERCOMMITMENT

Overcommitment is the result of not being able to say no to others. You become overwhelmed with outside commitments at work, church, in the community, and helping friends and distant relatives with projects.

How this sabotages your life: The people in your family, or those with whom you have significant close relationships, face quite a challenge when phrasing an everyday request, if they are sensitive and do not wish to overwhelm you. They may keep quiet about their own needs and wants because they can see how overwhelmed you already are. Also, it is lonely and painful for others to be shut out of your life while you are whirling around trying to meet all unnecessary commitments you made because you couldn't say no.

WHAT TO DO

Use the following space to describe how overcommitment operates in your life, if it does. Use these questions as a guideline for writing about it:

1. How does overcommitment harm you and keep you from being in recovery?

2. How does it affect others adversely and block intimacy?

3. Are you ready to have the Higher Power remove your compulsion to overcommit and learn to live without it?

4. If not, what are you gaining by holding on to it?

How Overcommitment Operates in My Life

1. **How does overcommitment harm you and keep you from being in recovery?**

2. **How does it affect others adversely and block intimacy?**

3. **Are you ready to have the Higher Power remove your compulsion to overcommit and learn to live without it?**

4. **If not, what are you gaining by holding on to it?**

PHYSICAL OR MENTAL ILLNESS

When you are overwhelmed with too many obligations, the resulting stress can create physical symptoms or mental conditions such as depression or irritability. Often you do not acknowledge these symptoms but inflict the consequences of them on people close to you. You may ignore symptoms that warn of more serious illnesses until those illnesses develop—painful debilitating ones such as allergies or arthritis, or life-threatening ones such as cancer and heart disease.

How this sabotages your life: The people close to you must endure your irritability and give you space to recover from the stress of illness. Your illness may require them to spend time, energy, and money on your care and on taking care of the things that you can't do because you are sick. And when you have your heart attack, develop your cancer, creep around in agony with your arthritis, drag through days and weeks of depression, allergies, and so on, you are not able to be physically available in your relationships.

WHAT TO DO

Use the following space to describe how physical or mental illness operates in your life, if it does. Use these questions as a guideline for writing about it:

1. How does your physical or mental condition harm you and keep you from being in recovery?

2. How does the stress of dealing with it affect others adversely and block intimacy?

3. Are you ready to have the Higher Power remove it and learn to live without it?

4. If not, what are you gaining by holding on to it?

How Physical or Mental Illness Operates in My Life

1. **How does your physical or mental condition harm you and keep you from being in recovery?**

2. **How does the stress of dealing with it affect others adversely and block intimacy?**

3. **Are you ready to have the Higher Power remove it and learn to live without it?**

4. **If not, what are you gaining by holding on to it?**

TOLERATING SEXUAL ABUSE
AND LOSS OF PERSONAL MORALITY

With damaged or nonexistent sexual boundaries, you may not be able to be faithful to your spouse or significant other sexually. (Being a sex addict and sexual offender is discussed in Step Four. This section is about being in the victim stance sexually.)

A separate issue from infidelity is tolerating sexual abuse from the person to whom you are committed to be faithful. This includes not being able to say no when your partner asks you to do sexual acts that are uncomfortable or painful, embarrassing, or against your moral code (for example, mate swapping, posing for pornographic pictures, and so on).

How this sabotages your life: A person living with a codependent who cannot be faithful sexually because of not being able to say no to inappropriate sexual advances is subjected to betrayal and faithlessness by someone he or she has loved and trusted. This is very painful. The unfaithful victim-codependent is subject to guilt and fear about not being responsible for his or her sexuality.

If you cannot say no to unpleasant sexual activities, your sexual partner is deceived into believing you enjoy them. You are subject to loss of personal comfort and dignity, along with possible physical injury. Also your level of respect for this partner may deteriorate, which seriously impairs your ability to relate to the person in a functional, loving, respectful manner. The deterioration of the relationship takes place without the other party knowing what the real cause is, giving that person no chance to deal with the real issues. The consequences are similar to those resulting from people-pleasing.

WHAT TO DO

Use the following space to describe how tolerating sexual abuse and the loss of personal morality operates in your life, if it does. Use these questions as a guideline for writing about it:

1. How does your inability to say no sexually harm you and keep you from being in recovery?

2. How does your inability to say no affect others adversely and block intimacy?

3. Are you ready to have the Higher Power remove the inability to say no and learn to live without it?

4. If not, what are you gaining by holding on to it?

How Tolerating Sexual Abuse Operates in My Life

1. How does your inability to say no sexually harm you and keep you from being in recovery?

2. How does your inability to say no affect others adversely and block intimacy?

3. Are you ready to have the Higher Power remove the inability to say no and learn to live without it?

4. If not, what are you gaining by holding on to it?

BLAMING OTHERS FOR YOUR REALITY AND TAKING RESPONSIBILITY FOR THE REALITY OF OTHERS

With damaged or nonexistent *internal* boundaries, you have reality in reverse, blaming other people for your own reality and taking responsibility for theirs. For example, you tell others that it's *their fault* that you are depressed (or angry, fearful, and so on). On the other hand, you may think that *you caused their* feelings or behavior. You interpret events with your skewed thinking, have skewed feelings, and blame the other person for your discomfort. Because of your own denial, you find it difficult to believe what the other person tells you about his or her own reality about the event.

How this sabotages your life: Living with a codependent who blames others for how he or she looks or what he or she is thinking, feeling, or choosing to do or not do (his or her reality) is painful and difficult. Every day it's as if the person living with you is walking through a mine field, waiting for blowups and attacks that cannot be avoided because he or she does not know how you are interpreting events, doing your skewed thinking, and then having inappropriate feelings about it.

WHAT TO DO

Use the following space to describe how blaming others for your reality and taking responsibility for theirs operates in your life, if it does. Use these questions as a guideline for writing about it:

1. How does blaming others for your reality and taking responsibility for theirs harm you and keep you from being in recovery?

2. How does this misplacing of responsibility for your own and others' reality affect others adversely and block intimacy?

3. Are you ready to have the Higher Power remove your blaming others and taking blame, and learn to live without it?

4. If not, what are you gaining by holding on to it?

How Misplacing Responsibility for My Own and Others' Reality Operates in My Life

1. How does blaming others for your reality and taking responsibility for theirs harm you and keep you from being in recovery?

2. How does this misplacing of responsibility for your own and others' reality affect others adversely and block intimacy?

3. Are you ready to have the Higher Power remove your blaming others and taking blame, and learn to live without it?

4. If not, what are you gaining by holding on to it?

INDECISIVENESS

With damaged or nonexistent intellectual boundaries, you have a very difficult time making decisions about the everyday events in your life. For example, an indecisive codependent might have difficulty deciding where to eat, what movie to see, or what suit to buy. Or another example might be as follows: A husband and wife agree on a certain policy about disciplining the children. But then the wife's mother comes for a visit and the mother has her own strong opinions that are different from those of the couple. The codependent wife changes her thinking and adopts her mother's opinions, opposing the husband. This is very painful for the husband.

How this sabotages your life: The person living or working with an indecisive codependent is subject to bafflement, frustration, anger, pain, and confusion when he or she experiences the codependent's changing from supporting the ideas the person presented to opposing them after being influenced by someone else.

WHAT TO DO

Use the following space to describe how indecisiveness operates in your life, if it does. Use these questions as a guideline for writing about it:

1. How does indecisiveness harm you and keep you from being in recovery?

2. How does indecisiveness affect others adversely and block intimacy?

3. Are you ready to have the Higher Power remove your indecisiveness and learn to live without it?

4. If not, what are you gaining by holding on to it?

How Indecisiveness Operates in My Life

1. How does indecisiveness harm you and keep you from being in recovery?

2. How does indecisiveness affect others adversely and block intimacy?

3. Are you ready to have the Higher Power remove your indecisiveness and learn to live without it?

4. If not, what are you gaining by holding on to it?

PUSHING OTHERS TO BE YOUR HIGHER POWER

When you cannot own your thinking very well, you often cannot make decisions about the everyday events in life. You expect the person with whom you are in relationship to come up with a decision and then you go along with it. But if you do not like the other person's decision, you often feel free to attack it or whine and complain that it isn't the right thing to do. When asked, you do not come up with a decision of your own.

How this sabotages your life: The other person finds himself or herself solely responsible for decisions and opinions on many family issues, such as child rearing, how to spend the money, whether to take the children to doctors, when to get the house repaired and whom to hire, where to go to church, and so on. This responsibility for decision making pushes that person toward the role of god or goddess of the relationship. The chosen decider is also subject to your criticism and attacks when you don't like the decision he or she made or it doesn't work out well.

WHAT TO DO

Use the following space to describe how pushing others to be your Higher Power operates in your life, if it does. Use these questions as a guideline for writing about it:

1. How does forcing others to make decisions affecting you harm you and keep you from being in recovery?

2. How does this opting out of taking the responsibility for deciding affect others adversely and block intimacy?

3. Are you ready to have the Higher Power remove this defect and learn to live without it?

4. If not, what are you gaining by holding on to it?

How Pushing Others to Be My Higher Power Operates in My Life

1. **How does forcing others to make decisions affecting you harm you and keep you from being in recovery?**

2. **How does this opting out of taking the responsibility for deciding affect others adversely and block intimacy?**

3. **Are you ready to have the Higher Power remove this defect and learn to live without it?**

4. **If not, what are you gaining by holding on to it?**

LACK OF PASSION

When you are at level B with your thinking or feelings, you cannot express an opinion or exhibit any feelings, including love and joy as well as the negative emotions, because you are not in touch with what your thinking or feelings really are.

How this sabotages your life: You can be perceived as boring in conversation because you never offer an opinion or risk disagreement. If you are at level B with your feelings and cannot identify them at all, you can be perceived by the other person as cold, nonaffectionate, impassionate, bland, and unexciting, which deprives the other person of a warm, intimate relationship.

WHAT TO DO

Use the following space to describe how being passionless (out of touch with your true thoughts and feelings) operates in your life, if it does. Use these questions as a guideline for writing about it:

1. How does your lack of passion harm you and keep you from being in recovery?

2. How does this passionless way of being affect others adversely and block intimacy?

3. Are you ready to have the Higher Power remove this defect and learn to live without it?

4. If not, what are you gaining by holding on to it?

How Lack of Passion Operates in My Life

1. How does your lack of passion harm you and keep you from being in recovery?

2. How does this passionless way of being affect others adversely and block intimacy?

3. Are you ready to have the Higher Power remove this defect and learn to live without it?

4. If not, what are you gaining by holding on to it?

Expressing Feelings Explosively

At the other extreme, the inability to own your feelings directly leads to occasional experiences of explosive feelings. After months of being "nice" and not angry, you may explode in rage over something that would ordinarily be only irritating. You may sink into deep depression or suicidal thoughts after trying to avoid owning your own pain. You may experience panic attacks as a result of not directly owning your fear.

How this sabotages your life: When your feelings erupt with great accumulated force at unexpected times, the people with whom you are in relationship are wounded and startled, making life with you a very uneasy or even frightening process.

What To Do

Use the following space to describe how expressing feelings explosively operates in your life, if it does. Use these questions as a guideline for writing about it:

1. How does this explosiveness harm you and keep you from being in recovery?

2. How does it affect others adversely and block intimacy?

3. Are you ready to have the Higher Power remove this defect and learn to live without it?

4. If not, what are you gaining by holding on to it?

How Expressing Feelings Explosively Operates in My Life

1. **How does this explosiveness harm you and keep you from being in recovery?**

2. **How does it affect others adversely and block intimacy?**

3. **Are you ready to have the Higher Power remove this defect and learn to live without it?**

4. **If not, what are you gaining by holding on to it?**

CONTROLLING THE REALITY OF OTHERS

When you cannot accept that your thinking is inaccurate, you cannot tolerate anyone who indicates that this might be so. If someone challenges a statement you have made, or merely expresses the fact that he or she doesn't agree, you begin to explain to the disputer why he or she is wrong and you are right, which is telling this person what to think (a form of controlling his or her reality).

How this sabotages your life: The person who disagrees with you suffers from being misjudged, falsely accused, and attacked for nonoffensive expressions of his or her honest feelings or thoughts, because of your inability to examine and own the possible inaccuracy of your own thinking.

WHAT TO DO

Use the following space to describe how controlling the reality of others operates in your life, if it does. Use these questions as a guideline for writing about it:

1. How does trying to get others to see things the way you do harm you and keep you from being in recovery?

2. How does this not tolerating differences of opinion without being threatened affect others adversely and block intimacy?

3. Are you ready to have the Higher Power remove this defect and learn to live without it?

4. If not, what are you gaining by holding on to it?

How Controlling the Reality of Others Operates in My Life

1. How does trying to get others to see things the way you do harm you and keep you from being in recovery?

2. How does this not tolerating differences of opinion without being threatened affect others adversely and block intimacy?

3. Are you ready to have the Higher Power remove this defect and learn to live without it?

4. If not, what are you gaining by holding on to it?

Lying, Dishonesty, Untrustworthiness

When you cannot own what you have done or not done, you invent stories about your behavior and tell them to the people you relate to. For example, if you forget to mail a letter on the way to work, when asked about it you may either say you did mail it (when you didn't) or say "I don't remember." Also, lying can be the result of distorting the reality of any situation to get what you want without having to say directly what it is. For example, you may have a mild headache, but claim your head is "splitting" to get your spouse to bring you dinner in bed.

How this sabotages your life: Your lying subjects other people to confusion, doubt, and mistrust of you in the relationship. When confronted directly, you are apt to lie or say "I don't remember" to cover up reality.

WHAT TO DO

Use the following space to describe how lying, dishonesty, or untrustworthiness operates in your life, if it does. Use these questions as a guideline for writing about it:

1. How does telling "white" (or regular) lies harm you and keep you from being in recovery?

2. How does lying or untrustworthiness affect others adversely and block intimacy?

3. Are you ready to have the Higher Power remove this defect and learn to live without it?

4. If not, what are you gaining by holding on to it?

How Lying, Dishonesty, or Untrustworthiness Operates in My Life

1. How does telling "white" (or regular) lies harm you and keep you from being in recovery?

2. How does lying or untrustworthiness affect others adversely and block intimacy?

3. Are you ready to have the Higher Power remove this defect and learn to live without it?

4. If not, what are you gaining by holding on to it?

HELPLESSNESS
(OVERWHELMING OTHERS
WITH YOUR NEEDS AND WANTS)

If you are in the position of being too needy and dependent, you place a huge and inappropriate burden on other people in your life to meet your needs, a responsibility that does not legitimately belong to others.

How this sabotages your life: This may create one or more of several difficulties for other people. They may experience inadequacy and guilt at not being able to meet your needs. They may need to back off and escape such a huge responsibility, which means they cannot be in an intimate relationship with you because of the need to keep distance for protection. They may experience pain when you react with resentment because they are not meeting all your needs.

WHAT TO DO

Use the following space to describe how helplessness operates in your life, if it does. Use these questions as a guideline for writing about it:

1. How does being helpless harm you and keep you from being in recovery?

2. How does your helplessness affect others adversely and block intimacy?

3. Are you ready to have the Higher Power remove this defect and learn to live without it?

4. If not, what are you gaining by holding on to it?

How Helplessness Operates in My Life

1. How does being helpless harm you and keep you from being in recovery?

2. How does your helplessness affect others adversely and block intimacy?

3. Are you ready to have the Higher Power remove this defect and learn to live without it?

4. If not, what are you gaining by holding on to it?

SHUTTING OTHERS OUT

If you are in the position of being *antidependent*, you know what your needs and wants are but refuse to ask for help when appropriate or to find out how to properly meet them.

If you are in a position of being *needless and wantless*, you are not even aware of some or all of your needs and wants. You may not eat properly, which affects your health and subjects other people to dealing with you while you are physically ill. You may not know you need physical and emotional nurturing from your mate.

How this sabotages your life: The person to whom you relate intimately may believe that he or she does not satisfy your need for, say, physical nurturing (hugs, affectionate physical contact) or sex or emotional nurturing (time, attention, and direction) or companionship. You shut the person out of being able to satisfy the basic dependency needs and wants that last all your life. And you also deprive the person of the opportunity to give intimacy to you, which is half of the process of intimacy.

WHAT TO DO   Use the following space to describe how being either antidependent or needless and wantless operates in your life, if it does. Use these questions as a guideline for writing about it:

1. How does the "I'll do it myself" or the "I'm OK, I don't need anything or anybody" stance harm you and keep you from being in recovery?

2. How does your shutting others out affect others adversely and block intimacy?

3. Are you ready to have the Higher Power remove this defect and learn to live without it?

4. If not, what are you gaining by holding on to it?

How Shutting Others Out Operates in My Life

1. How does the "I'll do it myself" or the "I'm OK, I don't need anything or anybody" stance harm you and keep you from being in recovery?

2. How does your shutting others out affect others adversely and block intimacy?

3. Are you ready to have the Higher Power remove this defect and learn to live without it?

4. If not, what are you gaining by holding on to it?

Inappropriate Social Behavior

You may not know how to dress properly, or refuse to do so even though you know how. You may not know correct social procedures or manners in certain social situations, or you may know but be unable or unwilling to follow these procedures. Or you could be in an antidependent state and try to guess at what correct social procedures are without asking for help and information, guessing wrong but not knowing it.

How this sabotages your life: When you neglect your clothing needs, the significant others in your life may experience shame or embarrassment about your inadequate or inappropriate clothing (the shame you would feel if you realized how inappropriate your clothing was). This can especially apply to your children if you do not know how to dress them appropriately and set them up for ridicule or shame when they go to school or out to play in the inadequate or inappropriate clothing you provide.

The other people around you must also cope with their feelings about you as you fail to hold up your end of the relationship in social situations such as entertaining at home, going to the boss's house for dinner, or going to a restaurant with friends.

WHAT TO DO

Use the following space to describe how inappropriate social behavior operates in your life, if it does. Use these questions as a guideline for writing about it:

1. How does not knowing or being unwilling to find out what is appropriate, or not being willing to do it, harm you and keep you from being in recovery?

2. How does social ignorance or failure to do your part affect others adversely and block intimacy?

3. Are you ready to have the Higher Power remove this defect and learn to live without it?

4. If not, what are you gaining by holding on to it?

How Inappropriate Social Behavior Operates in My Life

1. How does not knowing or being unwilling to find out what is appropriate, or not being willing to do it, harm you and keep you from being in recovery?

2. How does social ignorance or failure to do your part affect others adversely and block intimacy?

3. Are you ready to have the Higher Power remove this defect and learn to live without it?

4. If not, what are you gaining by holding on to it?

IRRESPONSIBILITY

You are irresponsible if you are not doing your share of day-to-day chores at home. You may not know how to establish and maintain appropriate living space.

How this sabotages your life: The people with whom you share a home then may have the full responsibility of making the home, or they must live in a substandard (dirty, underfurnished, dangerous) environment. This can be especially painful and harmful to your children, who depend on you to provide them with and teach them how to care for appropriate, clean, safe housing. (We are not talking about poverty-stricken parents with no income. We are discussing the fact that many people who live in dirty, substandard places could keep these places clean and repaired.)

WHAT TO DO

Use the following space to describe how irresponsibility operates in your life, if it does. Use these questions as a guideline for writing about it:

1. How does your irresponsibility concerning how to establish and maintain your living space harm you and keep you from being in recovery?

2. How does it affect others adversely and block intimacy?

3. Are you ready to have the Higher Power remove this defect and learn to live without it?

4. If not, what are you gaining by holding on to it?

How Irresponsibility Operates in My Life

1. How does your irresponsibility concerning how to establish and maintain your living space harm you and keep you from being in recovery?

2. How does it affect others adversely and block intimacy?

3. Are you ready to have the Higher Power remove this defect and learn to live without it?

4. If not, what are you gaining by holding on to it?

INADEQUATE AND UNFULFILLING SEX LIFE

You may have sexual problems that could be worked out if you were aware of them or if you would get help. But because you are not aware, or because you are ashamed of not knowing what to do in this area, you won't get help and continue to live with an inadequate and unfulfilling sex life.

How this sabotages your life: Your mate is deprived of a satisfying sex life with you, and the resulting resentment, frustration, and disappointment can color your entire relationship.

WHAT TO DO

Use the following space to describe how an inadequate and unfulfilling sex life affects you, if it does. Use these questions as a guideline for writing about it:

1. How does not dealing with your sexual problems harm you and keep you from being in recovery?

2. How does not facing your sexual issues affect others adversely and block intimacy?

3. Are you ready to have the Higher Power remove your ignorance or fear of getting help and learn to live without it?

4. If not, what are you gaining by holding on to it?

How an Inadequate and Unfulfilling Sex Life Affects Me

1. How does not dealing with your sexual problems harm you and keep you from being in recovery?

2. How does not facing your sexual issues affect others adversely and block intimacy?

3. Are you ready to have the Higher Power remove your ignorance or fear of getting help and learn to live without it?

4. If not, what are you gaining by holding on to it?

FINANCIAL PROBLEMS

You may not be aware of how to deal with money appropriately. You may overspend or refuse to spend enough to have the basic necessities for living plus enjoying meeting some wants.

How this sabotages your life: Not addressing financial responsibility subjects the people around you to either fear of going bankrupt because of your overspending or, at the other extreme, fear of your anger if they buy even the necessities for living.

WHAT TO DO

Use the following space to describe the financial problems in your life, if there are any. Use these questions as a guideline for writing about them:

1. How do financial worries or careless spending harm you and keep you from being in recovery?

2. How do problems stemming from or blamed on financial difficulties affect others adversely and block intimacy?

3. Are you ready to have the Higher Power remove this fear or financial irresponsibility and learn to live without it?

4. If not, what are you gaining by holding on to it?

How Financial Problems Affect Me

1. How do financial worries or careless spending harm you and keep you from being in recovery?

2. How do problems stemming from or blamed on financial difficulties affect others adversely and block intimacy?

3. Are you ready to have the Higher Power remove this fear or financial irresponsibility and learn to live without it?

4. If not, what are you gaining by holding on to it?

EXTREME PROBLEM SOLVING

If you are operating in extremes, you may fail to check out things that happen in a relationship by asking the other person to tell you his or her thinking and feelings related to the event or behavior. You also may not share your own extreme thinking. You often just burst out with your exaggerated feelings immediately following the event and then behave extremely. For example, if it appears you have been hurt by someone you love, you may solve the problem by stalking out, or by leaving the relationship altogether instead of sharing your pain and trying to reach an understanding with the other person.

How this sabotages your life: The other person in such a relationship never knows what to expect from you next. Your behavior is often baffling and painful, and when the person tries to find out what is behind it, your explanations seem bizarre. The other person may believe himself or herself to be falsely accused, misunderstood, or attacked for no apparent reason, and feel anger and pain about it. And your frequent threats to end the relationship leave the person fearful and unsure of your commitment.

WHAT TO DO

Use the following space to describe how extreme problem solving operates in your life, if it does. Use these questions as a guideline for writing about it:

1. How does extreme problem solving harm you and keep you from being in recovery?

2. How does it affect others adversely and block intimacy?

3. Are you ready to have the Higher Power remove this defect and learn to live without it?

4. If not, what are you gaining by holding on to it?

How Extreme Problem Solving Operates in My Life

1. **How does extreme problem solving harm you and keep you from being in recovery?**

2. **How does it affect others adversely and block intimacy?**

3. **Are you ready to have the Higher Power remove this defect and learn to live without it?**

4. **If not, what are you gaining by holding on to it?**

LACK OF INTIMACY

Intimacy requires sharing your thinking and feelings, but as we have seen, as a codependent you may act on extreme thinking and feelings without sharing them.

How this sabotages your life: The person in relationship with you is deprived of giving or receiving intimacy with you, and also deprived of any chance of developing an intimate relationship with you.

WHAT TO DO

Use the following space to describe how lack of intimacy operates in your life, if it does. Use these questions as a guideline for writing about it:

1. How does not sharing or not listening without judging harm you and keep you from being in recovery?

2. How do these affect others adversely and block intimacy?

3. Are you ready to have the Higher Power remove these blocks to intimacy and learn to live without them?

4. If not, what are you gaining by holding on to them?

How Lack of Intimacy Operates in My Life

1. How does not sharing or not listening without judging harm you and keep you from being in recovery?

2. How do these affect others adversely and block intimacy?

3. Are you ready to have the Higher Power remove these blocks to intimacy and learn to live without them?

4. If not, what are you gaining by holding on to them?

SCOREKEEPING

Scorekeeping involves observing and storing in your memory hurtful or imperfect things that other people have done. Then, when you are confronted for doing similar things, you can shift the focus off of your own imperfection onto theirs by reciting your scorecard about them or by pointing your finger and saying, "Well, you did it too—last Saturday at the supermarket!" The threat of such finger pointing blocks communication.

How this sabotages your life: The other person in such a relationship is prevented from sharing his or her thoughts and feelings about you with you. The fact that the person is also imperfect has little to do with the fact that your imperfection is the focus of his or her discomfort. It often happens very quickly in such a relationship that both parties cease any sort of personal sharing that could conceivably make them vulnerable to attack or counterattack. This process sabotages intimacy.

WHAT TO DO

Use the following space to describe how scorekeeping operates in your life, if it does. Use these questions as a guideline for writing about it:

1. How does keeping score harm you and keep you from being in recovery?

2. How does keeping score affect others adversely and block intimacy?

3. Are you ready to have the Higher Power remove scorekeeping and learn to live without it?

4. If not, what are you gaining by holding on to it?

How Scorekeeping Operates in My Life

1. How does keeping score harm you and keep you from being in recovery?

2. How does keeping score affect others adversely and block intimacy?

3. Are you ready to have the Higher Power remove scorekeeping and learn to live without it?

4. If not, what are you gaining by holding on to it?

JEALOUSY

I believe jealousy is a combination of shame and anger. When you are suffering from feeling less than others, you are subject to jealousy, believing that other people (who seem to be better than you are) are more interesting and attractive to your significant other. This green-eyed monster may well attack you without provocation, destroying your serenity and ability to give and receive intimacy.

How this sabotages your life: The other person is put through the experience of having to reassure you over and over again and may even go so far as to be extra careful not to do anything to trigger your jealousy. But the person is doomed to failure and experiences helplessness and hopelessness about the relationship every time you experience and express your jealousy.

WHAT TO DO

Use the following space to describe how jealousy operates in your life, if it does. Use these questions as a guideline for writing about it:

1. How does jealousy harm you and keep you from being in recovery?

2. How does being jealous affect others adversely and block intimacy?

3. Are you ready to have the Higher Power remove jealousy and learn to live without it?

4. If not, what are you gaining by holding on to it?

How Jealousy Operates in My Life

1. **How does jealousy harm you and keep you from being in recovery?**

2. **How does being jealous affect others adversely and block intimacy?**

3. **Are you ready to have the Higher Power remove jealousy and learn to live without it?**

4. **If not, what are you gaining by holding on to it?**

SELF-CENTEREDNESS

This character defect results from being so involved with your own problems, inadequacies, unmet expectations, overwhelming feelings, and other consequences of codependence that you are unwilling or unable to notice the impact of your behavior on other people.

How this sabotages your life: Other people often have the painful realization that while they can "be present" for you and support you through your miseries, you are unable to "be present" for them. After enough experiences of being let down by your inability to notice your impact on them, healthy people must turn to someone else who can "be there" for them.

WHAT TO DO

Use the following space to describe how self-centeredness operates in your life, if it does. Use these questions as a guideline for writing about it:

1. How does self-centered preoccupation harm you and keep you from being in recovery?

2. How does your self-centeredness affect others adversely and block intimacy?

3. Are you ready to have the Higher Power remove your self-centeredness and learn to live without it?

4. If not, what are you gaining by holding on to it?

How Self-Centeredness Operates in My Life

1. How does self-centered preoccupation harm you and keep you from being in recovery?

2. How does your self-centeredness affect others adversely and block intimacy?

3. Are you ready to have the Higher Power remove your self-centeredness and learn to live without it?

4. If not, what are you gaining by holding on to it?

INSISTING PEOPLE HAVE YOUR VALUE SYSTEM

Your inability to tolerate differences (due to a combination of codependence symptoms) means that you spend a lot of energy trying to convince the people in your life to live by the same values you do. Those who differ are met with disapproval, anger, and sometimes complete rejection.

How this sabotages your life: To be in relationship with you, other people must defend their own values, or pretend to agree with you when in fact they do not. Either situation is uncomfortable and can be dangerous to a person's integrity, since each person must face the consequences of his or her own decisions about values.

WHAT TO DO

Use the following space to describe how insisting people have your value system operates in your life, if it does. Use these questions as a guideline for writing about it:

1. How does insisting that others have your value system harm you and keep you from being in recovery?

2. How does it affect others adversely and block intimacy?

3. Are you ready to have the Higher Power remove this defect and learn to live without it?

4. If not, what are you gaining by holding on to it?

How Insisting People Have My Value System Operates in My Life

1. How does insisting that others have your value system harm you and keep you from being in recovery?

2. How does it affect others adversely and block intimacy?

3. Are you ready to have the Higher Power remove this defect and learn to live without it?

4. If not, what are you gaining by holding on to it?

ARGUING ABOUT FACTS AND
ALWAYS HAVING TO BE RIGHT (OR WRONG)

When it becomes evident that you and another person have different interpretations of an event, and that your idea of what is "right" or "true" does not agree with his or hers, you may move away from sharing thoughts and into arguing about what is really "right" or "true." This may seem similar to insisting that others have your value system, but the difference is that this defect is about the mental process each of you goes through to interpret the meaning of events. It may involve value systems or it may not.

This often accompanies the need to be right at all costs, which is a function of maintaining power or control in a relationship. It's as if you believe that being wrong would be a defeat of some kind, rather than a normal part of your imperfection. The other expression of having to have others agree with you is always giving in and being "wrong" in order to be taken care of by the other person.

How this sabotages your life: Other people experience unnecessary arguments with you and must defend their own interpretation of events, which interferes with the intimate process of simply hearing your thoughts and sharing their own. When confronted by your need for power and control through always being right, other people must give in to your power position and "stuff" their feelings about it to have a relationship with you. A healthy person will not be able to tolerate this condition, which may result in stormy scenes or in the person's deciding to leave the relationship altogether.

WHAT TO DO

Use the following space to describe how arguing about facts operates in your life, if it does. Use these questions as a guideline for writing about it:

1. How does arguing about facts harm you and keep you from being in recovery?

2. How does arguing about facts in a disagreement affect others adversely and block intimacy?

3. Are you ready to have the Higher Power remove this defect and learn to live without it?

4. If not, what are you gaining by holding on to it?

How Arguing About Facts Operates in My Life

1. How does arguing about facts harm you and keep you from being in recovery?

2. How does arguing about facts in a disagreement affect others adversely and block intimacy?

3. Are you ready to have the Higher Power remove this defect and learn to live without it?

4. If not, what are you gaining by holding on to it?

OTHER CHARACTER DEFECTS

WHAT TO DO Use the following space to name any other character defects you have recognized during this step that have not yet been listed. Feel free to use your own wording in naming these defects. After giving each defect a name, answer the following questions about it:

1. How does it harm you and keep you from being in recovery?

2. How does it affect others adversely and block intimacy?

3. Are you ready to have the Higher Power remove it and learn to live without it?

4. If not, what are you gaining by holding on to it?

How Other Defects Operate in My Life

1. How does it harm you and keep you from being in recovery?

2. How does it affect others adversely and block intimacy?

3. Are you ready to have the Higher Power remove it and learn to live without it?

4. If not, what are you gaining by holding on to it?

Step Seven

PURPOSE OF EXERCISE

The purpose of Step Seven is to acknowledge that you have come to the place where you are ready to stop doing the things that your character defects list has shown that you do that interfere with your relationships to yourself, others, and a Higher Power and keep you from being in recovery and responsible for your own life. It is a maturing process.

BACKGROUND READING

Read the following paragraphs before doing the writing exercise for this step.

Steps One, Four, Five, and Six have given you the data you need for this step. You have discovered how specific character defects such as people-pleasing, jealousy, demanding perfection from yourself or another person, overcontrolling someone else's reality, lying, and so forth are affecting your life and the lives of others.

- Step Four had you look at how you have affected others by disrespecting their boundaries and authentically offending them.

- Step Five had you acknowledge how you have harmed others.

- Step Six had you look more closely at how you affect others through character defects.

- Step Seven recognizes that you are ready to release your character defects and learn a new way to live.

I don't believe you can do Step Seven until you have finally gotten in enough pain from the knowledge of how your character defects affect other people. Many people can do Steps Four, Five, and Six and know all their character defects, but not want to surrender them. I believe that it is only out of your own pain that you become ready to surrender.

In one sense, Step Seven is like Step Three, except that now you have more specific data. In Step Six you acknowledged the impact of your illness on others and yourself. This knowledge causes you pain, and it is this pain that brings you to the point where it isn't worth it to you any longer to stay the same. And so now you truly want to release those shortcomings.

Unlike Step Five, Step Seven can be done alone. It is an experience between you and your Higher Power. In your mind you talk to your Higher Power, saying something like this: "Okay, Higher Power, I have allowed myself to know about this character defect to the point where I am in pain about it. I am aware of how (1) it has adversely affected other people and (2) it is adversely affecting me. I can't stand the pain and I want to stop this behavior [or character defect]. Would you please remove it from me because I can't."

The main point of this step is to surrender and let go of the shortcoming. You are now willing to learn to live without it. You have done all you can do to eliminate it and now you are asking your Higher Power to take it.

Until it goes away, you can begin to change what you are able to about the defect, but you must be willing to learn to live with the character defect in your life, knowing you have surrendered it, and love yourself anyway, until it is removed.

WHAT TO DO

In the column on the left, name a shortcoming from your writing in Step Six. In the column on the right, describe a healthy substitute for it.

EXAMPLE

SHORTCOMING	HEALTHY SUBSTITUTE
Perfectionism about my housecleaning	Cleaning enough to look good at a glance but not strain over small dirty places. Invite Anne over for lunch and leave a couple of bits of clutter. Concentrate on sharing with Anne instead of worrying about whether my house is "perfectly" clean and what she is thinking about it.

Healthy Substitutes for My Shortcomings

SHORTCOMING	HEALTHY SUBSTITUTE

SHORTCOMING	HEALTHY SUBSTITUTE

SHORTCOMING	*HEALTHY SUBSTITUTE*

SHORTCOMING	HEALTHY SUBSTITUTE

SHORTCOMING	HEALTHY SUBSTITUTE

Step Eight

> *"Made a list of all persons we had harmed and became willing to make amends to them all."*

PURPOSE OF EXERCISE

The purpose of this step is to turn your focus from what has been done *to you* and toward what you have done *to others*.

BACKGROUND READING

Review what you have written in this workbook for Steps Four and Six. Note who is involved. In Step Four, note those people whose boundaries you have disregarded. In Step Six, note those people who have suffered from your character defects, even though you may not have disregarded their boundaries.

WHAT TO DO

First, list the names of people you have harmed, mentioned in Steps Four and Six, as well as any others you can think of at this time. Describe the specific incident(s) as completely as you can. Describe your part in the harm but *do not describe anything the other person did to you, whether before or after your harmful behavior.* The point of this step is to look at your own harmful behavior without justification, defenses, or excuses. Give the approximate date (year only or year and month) of the incident(s). Leave the last space labeled "What I would do to make amends" blank for the moment.

EXAMPLE

NAME: Carole   **APPROX. DATE:** Spring 1978
WHAT I DID: I refused to speak to her after a certain encounter. I snubbed her at an office party and hung up on her twice during that time. Later, I spoke to her but have remained cool and distant ever since.
WHAT I WOULD DO TO MAKE AMENDS:
(To be filled in later.)

NAME: Joseph   **APPROX. DATE:** 1979
WHAT I DID: We dated for a year. I lied to him about dating other men. He preferred me not to date and I didn't see any harm in it. Rather than bring out this difference of thinking, I chose to avoid a fight by lying. He found out and told me. I accused him of being a spy and broke up with him, never speaking to him again. I'd rather have lost him altogether than face negotiating this difference between us.
WHAT I WOULD DO TO MAKE AMENDS:
(To be filled in later.)

People I Have Harmed and the Amends I Could Make

1. **NAME:**   **APPROX. DATE:**
   WHAT I DID:

   WHAT I WOULD DO TO MAKE AMENDS:

2. **NAME:**   **APPROX. DATE:**
   WHAT I DID:

   WHAT I WOULD DO TO MAKE AMENDS:

3. **NAME:**   **APPROX. DATE:**
   WHAT I DID:

   WHAT I WOULD DO TO MAKE AMENDS:

4. **NAME:**   **APPROX. DATE:**
   WHAT I DID:

   WHAT I WOULD DO TO MAKE AMENDS:

5. NAME: **APPROX. DATE:**

WHAT I DID:

WHAT I WOULD DO TO MAKE AMENDS:

6. NAME: **APPROX. DATE:**

WHAT I DID:

WHAT I WOULD DO TO MAKE AMENDS:

7. NAME: **APPROX. DATE:**
  WHAT I DID:

  WHAT I WOULD DO TO MAKE AMENDS:

8. NAME: **APPROX. DATE:**
  WHAT I DID:

  WHAT I WOULD DO TO MAKE AMENDS:

9. NAME: **APPROX. DATE:**

    WHAT I DID:

    WHAT I WOULD DO TO MAKE AMENDS:

10. NAME: **APPROX. DATE:**

    WHAT I DID:

    WHAT I WOULD DO TO MAKE AMENDS:

11. NAME: **APPROX. DATE:**
    WHAT I DID:

    WHAT I WOULD DO TO MAKE AMENDS:

12. NAME: **APPROX. DATE:**
    WHAT I DID:

    WHAT I WOULD DO TO MAKE AMENDS:

13. NAME: **APPROX. DATE:**
    WHAT I DID:

    WHAT I WOULD DO TO MAKE AMENDS:

14. NAME: **APPROX. DATE:**
    WHAT I DID:

    WHAT I WOULD DO TO MAKE AMENDS:

15. NAME: APPROX. DATE:
　　WHAT I DID:

WHAT I WOULD DO TO MAKE AMENDS:

16. NAME: APPROX. DATE:
　　WHAT I DID:

WHAT I WOULD DO TO MAKE AMENDS:

17. **NAME:**   **APPROX. DATE:**
    WHAT I DID:

    WHAT I WOULD DO TO MAKE AMENDS:

18. **NAME:**   **APPROX. DATE:**
    WHAT I DID:

    WHAT I WOULD DO TO MAKE AMENDS:

The second half of Step Eight is to become willing to make amends to each person. Even though you may not be willing to make amends at this point, go back to your list and write some ideas about how you might approach the person if you were willing to make amends.

EXAMPLE	

NAME: Carole
WHAT I WOULD DO TO MAKE AMENDS: I would call Carole to ask her to lunch. If she accepted, I would tell her at lunch that I was wrong to treat her so rudely and that I've missed her friendship and am sorry I cut it off. If she declined to go to lunch, I would tell her these things right then on the telephone.

NAME: Joseph
WHAT I WOULD DO TO MAKE AMENDS: I would write Joseph a letter since he lives in another state and tell him I was wrong to lie to him and then not own up to it when he confronted me. I would admit fully that I had lied on purpose to avoid a confrontation with him and that I feel shame and pain about not being honest with him.

Step Nine

> *"Made direct amends to such people wherever possible, except when to do so would injure them or others."*

The purpose of Step Nine is for you to repair the damage you did in the past, so that you can grow toward increasing maturity. It is an exercise in how to be appropriately accountable for the part of your "perfect imperfection" that has caused harm to others.

BACKGROUND READING

Read the following paragraphs before doing this exercise.

Making amends is more than an apology. It usually means that you acknowledge specifically what happened, make a commitment to the offended person not to do it anymore, and carry out that commitment to the best of your ability. This is the primary meaning and is the preferred method of completing this step (when it would not injure the person or other people in his or her life or yourself). You can make amends by visiting the person to talk to him or her, by talking to him or her over the telephone, or by writing him or her a letter.

The reason you make direct amends to people you have harmed is so that you can recover from your illness of codependence. The primary purpose of making amends is *not* to repair a broken relation between you and the other person. If the relationship does get mended, that is merely a happy by-product of doing the step. But whatever *the other person's reaction* to your amends, you have succeeded if you have cleared off *your* side of the street.

It is important to remember that after you have made your direct amends, the other person is very likely to have a response. You stay in recovery when you can simply listen and observe the response, letting the person be whoever he or she is. The response may be a "thank you," or it may be criticism and anger. The other person's response is not relevant to the reason for doing this step.

It is entirely possible that the person you make amends to cannot forgive you or is not willing to restore the relationship between you for reasons of his or her own. If this is true, you can still achieve your goals: practicing appropriate accountability toward others, gaining forgiveness from yourself and your Higher Power, and growing toward increasing maturity. Other people do not have the power to stop you from completing this step.

However, in cases in which making direct amends is impossible because it would harm the person or another person, or because the person has died, indirect amends can still be carried out. When people amend the constitution of an organization, they change it so it is improved. When you make indirect amends, you change your thinking, your attitudes, your judgments about people so that they are improved and more mature. You are now nonoffensive in the areas in which you were offensive before. You stop causing them to suffer for your shortcomings as you did before, or if you do cause them to suffer, you find ways to make restitution other than direct amends.

An example of a case in which making direct amends would harm the person or another person is when someone has an affair with a married person. Let's say a man has an affair with a married woman (although, of course, we could as easily imagine a woman having an affair with a married man).

This man is now doing Steps Eight and Nine, so he lists the woman he had the affair with and her husband. He knows that the woman ended the affair and continued her marriage, choosing not to tell her husband about the affair. The marriage is going well. If the offending man were to go to the husband to make amends for having had an affair with his wife, both the husband and the wife would be harmed. Making indirect amends is more appropriate.

Depending on his present attitudes, thinking, feelings, or behaviors, here are some options the offending man can choose. If he has had an attitude of "Well, she wanted it as much as I did, so I'm not responsible. It was just one of those things," he can amend his attitude and be willing to feel the pain, shame, and guilt associated with this external and internal boundary violation. He can grieve for it, offer it to the Higher Power, and share the feelings with a safe, trusted third party. This experiencing the emotional consequences of his behavior can give him the wisdom, humility, and accountability to help him avoid similar boundary violations in the future.

If he has continued to try to contact the woman, ignoring her protests, he can amend his behavior and leave her alone. If he entered the affair because of thinking all women are merely sexual targets and this one was "an easy lay," he can amend his thinking and stop believing he is superior to women, or to *that* woman in particular, and can acknowledge that this woman and other women have value equal to him, requiring respect.

These are just a few examples of how this man could make indirect amends for his affair without going to the woman or her husband directly. He, himself, would gain recovery by becoming amended—changed and different.

Therefore, it is important to consider making indirect amends if direct amends would injure the person or others.

Another part of this step involves offering restitution in addition to amends whenever your harmful action has taken something of value away from someone. To make restitution means you repay the person in like kind (or as close as possible) for whatever has been lost.

You may have failed to repay a loan; you may have lost, destroyed, or damaged someone's property by physical violence or carelessness; you may have caused someone to spend time righting the wrong you did; you may have made it necessary for someone to spend extra time doing something that could have been done faster except for your interference; you may have promised to help someone do something, then failed to do so, leaving the person to do the task alone. To make restitution you would arrange a schedule to repay money and then make each payment on time; repair or replace damaged property; or offer your time to help out with something such as free baby-sitting, lawn mowing, running errands, or something else the person needs to have done.

WHAT TO DO

List in the following space the people you named in Step Eight, and decide whether direct amends would injure them or not.

PEOPLE I HAVE HARMED NAME	WOULD DIRECT AMENDS INJURE?	
	YES	NO

List in the following space people you named in Step Eight who have died.

PEOPLE I HAVE HARMED WHO HAVE DIED:

Now go ahead and make direct amends to those people who would not be harmed. As you make amends, list in the following space the name, date, and what action you took to make amends and/or restitution to each person. Note also any feelings you had as you made amends.

| EXAMPLE |

NAME: Carole   **DATE:** Jan. 1989
HOW I MADE AMENDS: I invited her to lunch, she accepted. I told her face to face that I had seen how wrong and rude I had been to her starting back in 1978 and I wanted her to know that I had realized it. I told her I wanted to stop treating her this way and promised to stop. I told her I now felt ashamed and also sad that I had not been a friend to her over the years and that I had thought of her often and missed her.

HOW I MADE RESTITUTION, IF NECESSARY: Carole was surprised, then angry. She told me how she had felt and how stuck-up she thought I was. I held my tongue and listened to her without commenting. As she talked, I felt pain to see how my attitude, pride, and behavior had hurt her. I did not mention what she had done that I had reacted to—and neither did she. But when she finished I thanked her for telling me these things and we both left. I don't know what will happen next in our relationship, but I could tell I was different with her.

Direct Amends I Have Made

1. **NAME:**   **DATE:**
   HOW I MADE AMENDS:

   HOW I MADE RESTITUTION, IF NECESSARY:

2. **NAME:**   **DATE:**
   HOW I MADE AMENDS:

   HOW I MADE RESTITUTION, IF NECESSARY:

3. NAME: **DATE:**

HOW I MADE AMENDS:

HOW I MADE RESTITUTION, IF NECESSARY:

4. NAME: **DATE:**

HOW I MADE AMENDS:

HOW I MADE RESTITUTION, IF NECESSARY:

5. NAME: **DATE:**

HOW I MADE AMENDS:

HOW I MADE RESTITUTION, IF NECESSARY:

6. NAME: **DATE:**

HOW I MADE AMENDS:

HOW I MADE RESTITUTION, IF NECESSARY:

7. NAME: **DATE:**

   HOW I MADE AMENDS:

   HOW I MADE RESTITUTION, IF NECESSARY:

8. NAME: **DATE:**

   HOW I MADE AMENDS:

   HOW I MADE RESTITUTION, IF NECESSARY:

9. **NAME:**   **DATE:**

   HOW I MADE AMENDS:

   HOW I MADE RESTITUTION, IF NECESSARY:

10. **NAME:**   **DATE:**

    HOW I MADE AMENDS:

    HOW I MADE RESTITUTION, IF NECESSARY:

11. NAME: **DATE:**

HOW I MADE AMENDS:

HOW I MADE RESTITUTION, IF NECESSARY:

12. NAME: **DATE:**

HOW I MADE AMENDS:

HOW I MADE RESTITUTION, IF NECESSARY:

13. NAME: **DATE:**

HOW I MADE AMENDS:

HOW I MADE RESTITUTION, IF NECESSARY:

14. NAME: **DATE:**

HOW I MADE AMENDS:

HOW I MADE RESTITUTION, IF NECESSARY:

15. NAME: **DATE:**
     HOW I MADE AMENDS:

     HOW I MADE RESTITUTION, IF NECESSARY:

16. NAME: **DATE:**
     HOW I MADE AMENDS:

     HOW I MADE RESTITUTION, IF NECESSARY:

To complete this step, make indirect amends to those people who would be injured by a direct acknowledgment of what happened or who have died. As you make indirect amends, describe in the following space what you did and how you are now amended in attitude, judgment, thinking, feelings, or behavior.

EXAMPLE

NAME: Joseph　　　　　　　　**DATE:** Feb. 1989
WHY INDIRECT AMENDS ARE NECESSARY: Joseph died 5 years ago.
WHAT I DID AND HOW I AM AMENDED: I wrote a letter to him anyway and in the process got in touch with my feelings of guilt, shame, and pain about my lying to him. I allowed myself to feel the feelings. I read the letter to my sponsor and shared these feelings with her. I see how my lies hurt people. I think after feeling all this guilt, shame, and pain I will think hard before I lie like that again, and should I realize I have lied, I will admit and acknowledge it much sooner!

Indirect Amends I Have Made

1. NAME: **DATE:**

   WHY INDIRECT AMENDS ARE NECESSARY:

   WHAT I DID AND HOW I AM AMENDED:

2. NAME: **DATE:**

   WHY INDIRECT AMENDS ARE NECESSARY:

   WHAT I DID AND HOW I AM AMENDED:

3. NAME: **DATE:**

WHY INDIRECT AMENDS ARE NECESSARY:

WHAT I DID AND HOW I AM AMENDED:

4. NAME: **DATE:**

WHY INDIRECT AMENDS ARE NECESSARY:

WHAT I DID AND HOW I AM AMENDED:

5. **NAME:**   **DATE:**
   WHY INDIRECT AMENDS ARE NECESSARY:

   WHAT I DID AND HOW I AM AMENDED:

6. **NAME:**   **DATE:**
   WHY INDIRECT AMENDS ARE NECESSARY:

   WHAT I DID AND HOW I AM AMENDED:

7. NAME: DATE:

WHY INDIRECT AMENDS ARE NECESSARY:

WHAT I DID AND HOW I AM AMENDED:

8. NAME: DATE:

WHY INDIRECT AMENDS ARE NECESSARY:

WHAT I DID AND HOW I AM AMENDED:

9. NAME: **DATE:**
WHY INDIRECT AMENDS ARE NECESSARY:

WHAT I DID AND HOW I AM AMENDED:

10. NAME: **DATE:**
WHY INDIRECT AMENDS ARE NECESSARY:

WHAT I DID AND HOW I AM AMENDED:

11. NAME: **DATE:**

   WHY INDIRECT AMENDS ARE NECESSARY:

   WHAT I DID AND HOW I AM AMENDED:

12. NAME: **DATE:**

   WHY INDIRECT AMENDS ARE NECESSARY:

   WHAT I DID AND HOW I AM AMENDED:

13. NAME: **DATE:**

WHY INDIRECT AMENDS ARE NECESSARY:

WHAT I DID AND HOW I AM AMENDED:

14. NAME: **DATE:**

WHY INDIRECT AMENDS ARE NECESSARY:

WHAT I DID AND HOW I AM AMENDED:

15. NAME: **DATE:**

WHY INDIRECT AMENDS ARE NECESSARY:

WHAT I DID AND HOW I AM AMENDED:

16. NAME: **DATE:**

WHY INDIRECT AMENDS ARE NECESSARY:

WHAT I DID AND HOW I AM AMENDED:

Step Ten

"Continued to take personal inventory, and when we were wrong, promptly admitted it."

PURPOSE OF EXERCISE

The purpose of the exercise for Step Ten is to give you a way to keep track of how your codependence is still operating and how it continues to harm others or you.

Breaking free from denial about your *recovery* is just as important to your progress as breaking free from denial about being a codependent. Many codependents share the common trait of being unaware of progress they are making toward living in recovery rather than in codependence. This is a key step toward developing a life-style of recovery. Not only is it helpful to keep track of when you are wrong so you can promptly admit it, but it is also gratifying to see how you are changing in a functional direction as you respond to certain situations. The continual personal inventory this step calls for should include what went well along with what still needs improvement.

You may choose to do a nightly review of each day or a weekly review of the past week. Going longer than a week between reviews is not recommended.

If you have a particularly difficult day you may wish to do a review of the day that very night. If you find your life flowing better, you might wait to do the review until the end of the week. However, doing a nightly review of each day for the first few months even if your life is flowing well can give you valuable information about your progress in recovery. It is not necessary to wait until you have a painful encounter with someone to do this review, although it certainly helps to do such a review at those times.

You have already written your own guidelines for what to review about your life in Steps One, Four, Six, and Eight in this workbook, so you can begin to keep track of what is going on currently in these areas as you progress toward recovery. Space is provided for you to review each of these steps in your inventory. (When you have filled the space in this workbook for each step, continue to write in a separate notebook.)

REVIEW OF STEP ONE: POWERLESSNESS AND UNMANAGEABLE CONSEQUENCES

BACKGROUND READING

Read your description of yourself—your powerlessness over the five core symptoms and your experience of their unmanageable consequences—as written in Step One of this workbook.

WHAT TO DO

Reflect on the past day or week to discover whether you have experienced powerlessness over the core symptoms or the unmanageable consequences that you wrote about in Step One. Use the space following to describe what you discover.

My Recent Experiences of Core Symptoms or Consequences

1. **DATE:**
   CORE SYMPTOM OR UNMANAGEABLE CONSEQUENCE:

   WHAT HAPPENED:

2. **DATE:**
   CORE SYMPTOM OR UNMANAGEABLE CONSEQUENCE:

   WHAT HAPPENED:

3. **DATE:**

   CORE SYMPTOM OR UNMANAGEABLE CONSEQUENCE:

   WHAT HAPPENED:

4. **DATE:**

   CORE SYMPTOM OR UNMANAGEABLE CONSEQUENCE:

   WHAT HAPPENED:

5. **DATE:**
   CORE SYMPTOM OR UNMANAGEABLE CONSEQUENCE:

   WHAT HAPPENED:

6. **DATE:**
   CORE SYMPTOM OR UNMANAGEABLE CONSEQUENCE:

   WHAT HAPPENED:

REVIEW OF STEP FOUR:
HOW I DISREGARD THE BOUNDARIES OF OTHERS

BACKGROUND READING

Read your description of yourself and how you have disregarded the boundaries of others, as written in Step Four of this workbook.

WHAT TO DO

Reflect on the past day or week to discover whether you have been authentically offensive toward someone mentioned in Step Four, or someone not mentioned. Use the following space to describe any such offenses. (In Step Ten, you will probably be increasingly able to notice your offense sooner and make direct amends by acknowledging the offense to the person offended, if it would not harm him or her, and committing not to do it again.)

My Recent Boundary Offenses

1. NAME: **DATE:**
   OFFENSE I COMMITTED:

2. NAME: **DATE:**
   OFFENSE I COMMITTED:

3. NAME: **DATE:**
   OFFENSE I COMMITTED:

4. NAME: **DATE:**
   OFFENSE I COMMITTED:

5. NAME: **DATE:**
   OFFENSE I COMMITTED:

6. NAME: **DATE:**
   OFFENSE I COMMITTED:

REVIEW OF STEP SIX:
HOW OTHERS (AND I) SUFFER
FROM MY CHARACTER DEFECTS

BACKGROUND READING

Read your description of the specific character defects you discovered, as written in Step Six of this workbook. Remember, codependent character defects are attitudes, feelings, and behaviors that you hang on to that keep you from taking responsibility for your own life and recovery.

WHAT TO DO

Reflect on the past day or week to discover whether any character defects have been operating to keep you from taking responsibility for your own life and recovery. Use the following space to describe what happened. Also, write about any new character defect you have discovered since the last time you reviewed this aspect of your life.

My Recent Experiences with Character Defects

1. **CHARACTER DEFECT:**
   WHAT HAPPENED:

2. **CHARACTER DEFECT:**
   WHAT HAPPENED:

3. CHARACTER DEFECT:
   WHAT HAPPENED:

4. CHARACTER DEFECT:
   WHAT HAPPENED:

5. CHARACTER DEFECT:
   WHAT HAPPENED:

6. CHARACTER DEFECT:
   WHAT HAPPENED:

REVIEW OF STEP EIGHT:
THE PEOPLE I HARMED AND MADE AMENDS TO

BACKGROUND READING

Read your list of people you harmed, as written in Step Eight of this workbook.

WHAT TO DO

Reflect on the past day or week to discover whether any other incidents have occurred in which you have harmed (either in the same way or in a new way) any of the people you listed in Step Eight. If you discover any, promptly admit it to the person, if it would not harm him or her, and make restitution. Use the following space to describe any incidents that have occurred since the last time you reviewed this aspect of your life.

My Recent Offenses and Amends

1. NAME:
   WHAT HAPPENED:

2. NAME:
   WHAT HAPPENED:

3. NAME:
WHAT HAPPENED:

4. NAME:
WHAT HAPPENED:

5. NAME:
   WHAT HAPPENED:

6. NAME:
   WHAT HAPPENED:

Step Eleven

> *"Sought through prayer and meditation to improve our conscious contact with God, praying only for knowledge of God's will for us and the power to carry it out."*

PURPOSE OF EXERCISE

The main purpose of this step is for you to experience connectedness to your Higher Power. The purpose of the writing exercise for this step is to help you sharpen your spiritual awareness by acknowledging if and how that awareness is growing and developing. Once you have felt and written about your experience, you can read your writing later when you are in a time when it is hard to feel connected to your Higher Power.

BACKGROUND READING

The following paragraphs are about my own experience with this step. I share my experience here as an example of one person's journey with the hope that it may inspire your own search for a Higher Power. The step suggests that the two key ingredients of prayer and meditation are a common starting place for each of us.

PRAYER

In prayer, I do only one thing: ask for my Higher Power's will in my life. Essentially I ask my Higher Power to help me and be with me as I go through my day. At the beginning of my day I make a statement to myself that I'm willing to have my Higher Power's will in my life today and I'm willing to do my Higher Power's will as I am aware of it. I say a prayer, asking my Higher Power for its will for me and for the power to carry it out.

I connect with my Higher Power through meditation over my perfect imperfection. I also think about the positive things that I have been given or that have happened for which I am grateful. An attitude of gratefulness has been very important in breaking my denial about the positive things that have happened in my recovery and breaking my habit of dwelling on the negative aspects of my surroundings. I also connect with my Higher Power as I ask for its will in my life and start noticing the Higher Power's will and then doing it. My Step Eleven work with myself is a spiritual step because it does connect me to my Higher Power through meditation (embracing my perfect imperfection) and through prayer (asking for my Higher Power's will).

MEDITATION

I believe that for me as a codependent, meditation involves being quiet and allowing myself to know myself as a perfectly imperfect person. It is a time to listen to myself, to know where I have been and what I have been thinking. I try to balance the reality of my perfect imperfection with self-esteem, acknowledging that the imperfection is there and loving myself anyway. I feel joy about the fact that I am acceptable to myself and my Higher Power with my imperfection. I feel pain when I can acknowledge how my imperfection affects other people in a negative way. When I can both acknowledge my imperfection and love myself anyway, I am open to contact with the Higher Power. As I allow myself to feel joy or pain about my reality, at that moment I often notice that I am in a relationship with a power greater than myself. I feel myself connected to it.

I recognize that other people may meditate in different ways. I offer this to you as an exercise to do for a while to practice embracing your own imperfection without any accompanying self-punishment, anguish, or shame attacks.

WHAT TO DO

Once a week or every month or so, use the following space to write about your experiences with your Higher Power. Describe the times when you experience joy-filled pain or pain-filled joy, and the issue of perfect imperfection you are aware of when this happens.

My Experiences with My Own Imperfection

1. **DATE:**
   WHAT HAPPENED:

2. **DATE:**
   WHAT HAPPENED:

3. DATE:
  WHAT HAPPENED:

4. DATE:
  WHAT HAPPENED:

5. DATE:
 WHAT HAPPENED:

6. DATE:
 WHAT HAPPENED:

7. DATE:
   WHAT HAPPENED:

8. DATE:
   WHAT HAPPENED:

Describe the times you have been aware of the Higher Power's will in your life and how you were able to do it.

My Experiences with the Higher Power's Will

1. DATE:
   WHAT HAPPENED:

2. DATE:
   WHAT HAPPENED:

3. **DATE:**
   WHAT HAPPENED:

4. **DATE:**
   WHAT HAPPENED:

5. DATE:
    WHAT HAPPENED:

6. DATE:
    WHAT HAPPENED:

7. DATE:

   WHAT HAPPENED:

8. DATE:

   WHAT HAPPENED:

Step Twelve

PURPOSE OF EXERCISE

This step is a step of physical actions as well as mental, emotional, and spiritual ones. The purpose of the writing exercise is to help you recognize instances in which you carry the message or practice the principles of this program in some part of your life. Such recognition helps you break free from denial about your recovery in this area.

BACKGROUND READING

Before beginning to carry out this step, read the following paragraphs.

CARRYING THE MESSAGE OF CODEPENDENCE

Carrying the message of codependence involves confronting the disease in other people by sharing the evidence of the disease in ourselves. You can do this at meetings, by sharing what is going on with you and by chairing a meeting and identifying at a deeper level. It can also be done when someone you know brings up issues of codependence and child abuse in a conversation. You can point out your personal understanding of how codependence operates—not as it relates to the other person but as it relates to you. To confront codependence in other people in a direct attempt to change them is to be back in the disease of controlling other people's reality by trying to make them agree that they have problems with codependence and that they need help.

One of the ongoing ways to help carry the message is to participate in a Codependents Anonymous group. Being willing to speak up about what is going on with you, even when you are in a position of awareness of your imperfection, is part of carrying the message. Being willing to chair a meeting after you've attended enough meetings to qualify (according to whatever the guidelines are in your particular group) and taking part in other tasks that are necessary to keep a meeting going, such as setting up the room, cleaning up after a meeting, serving as group representative, treasurer, or other positions where service is needed—all these are part of carrying the message.

PRACTICING THESE PRINCIPLES IN ALL OUR AFFAIRS

Practicing these principles in all your affairs means you try to stay aware that you are a codependent and you are perfectly imperfect. This is a chronic condition that can return at any moment. You're only in remission from codependence when you are practicing recovery.

To practice these principles in all your affairs, you also must stay aware of the preceding eleven steps and how they specifically relate to this disease. Keep practicing all eleven steps in your daily living as appropriate. By doing these steps, your spirituality will develop.

WHAT TO DO

Use the following space to describe instances when you have carried the message by sharing how codependence operates for you.

How I Have Carried the Message

1. **DATE:**
   WHAT HAPPENED:

2. **DATE:**
   WHAT HAPPENED:

3. DATE:
    WHAT HAPPENED:

4. DATE:
    WHAT HAPPENED:

5. **DATE:**
   WHAT HAPPENED:

6. **DATE:**
   WHAT HAPPENED:

From time to time a situation will occur to which you respond in ways that evidence your recovery. Later you realize, "Hey, I was different that time. A year ago I would have had a much more codependent reaction to that!" Use the following space to write about such instances.

Evidence of My Recovery

1. **SITUATION:**
   MY RESPONSE:

2. **SITUATION:**
   MY RESPONSE:

3. SITUATION:
   MY RESPONSE:

4. SITUATION:
   MY RESPONSE:

Part 3

BEYOND DENIAL ABOUT YOUR RECOVERY

Introduction

As a codependent, you are likely to be in denial about recovery when it begins to happen. You can often see improvement in the lives of other recovering codependents while believing yourself to be stuck in the same old patterns of appearing, thinking, feeling, behaving. In this section you will write about recovery experiences regarding each core symptom. Writing about recovery helps break through your denial and fix the experiences in your conscious mind for a longer time. Such writing also makes these recovery experiences convenient to read about later when you need encouragement about your recovery process.

The purpose of this section is to guide you into developing the recovery traits related to each of the five symptoms: self-esteem from the inside, functional boundaries, ability to own your reality, ability to recognize and meet your own needs and wants, and living life in moderation. In the following pages you will find information and exercises about how to confront each of the five core symptoms you wrote about in Step One.

I strongly recommend that you work on one symptom at a time rather than trying to confront all five symptoms simultaneously. Recovery is a building process. The foundation is laid by establishing self-esteem. Once you begin to perceive your own value, you are better able to set boundaries because you now know you are worth protecting. With healthier boundaries you are more able to risk owning your own thoughts, feelings, and behavior, because you can protect yourself from being controlled by others who do not like your reality. And you can keep yourself from controlling others and living a "secondhand" life — someone else's. When you are more in touch with your reality, you are more aware of who you are and can tolerate your own imperfection. Therefore, you can start to identify and meet your own needs and wants. And you can begin to experience and express reality in moderation and to stop operating in extremes.

Addressing the symptoms in this order has worked well for me. As I write this, I am now improving my ability to experience and express myself moderately. But since recovery is a process, not an event, I sometimes am likely to "flap out there in the wild blue yonder," bouncing from one extreme to the other.

You will probably find that awareness of unmanageable consequences is easier to achieve than awareness of specific symptoms. When I began my recovery journey, I had more awareness of the results of my symptoms (how my codependence was creating unmanageable consequences in my life) than I did of the symptoms themselves. But try as I would, I could not seem to stop the self-sabotaging consequences: negative control, resentment, distorted spirituality, avoiding reality, and inability to sustain intimacy.

Recovery from these consequences was easier when I focused on the core symptoms that were creating powerlessness first. Afterward I found I could begin addressing the unmanageable consequences. This seems natural to me now, since I realize that it is because of the symptoms that I experience the harmful consequences. When the symptoms got better, the consequences decreased and I could more easily intervene in any that still existed after my symptoms had improved.

Here are the two keys to getting the most out of this section:

1. Work on one symptom at a time, in the order given.

2. Even though the *consequences* of your symptoms are easier to identify, work on recovery from the *symptoms* because this leads automatically to improvement in the consequences. Initially, put more emphasis on the core symptoms and focus on seeing how they create the unmanageable consequences. You will see how these consequences begin to improve as you begin to heal from the core symptoms.

Affirming Your Self-Esteem

Healthy self-esteem is the internal experience of your own preciousness, awareness from inside yourself that you have worth. This worth is separate from anything you do, how you look, or what other people in your life say or do to you or about you. An essential component of recovery from codependence is learning to sense your own value as a person.

PURPOSE OF EXERCISES

These exercises are to help you develop a sense of self-esteem neither lower nor higher than anyone else.

BACKGROUND READING

(1) Review pages 7–10 of *Facing Codependence,* about impaired self-esteem. (2) Review pages 77–80 of *Facing Codependence,* about a child's value in a dysfunctional family. (3) Review your own writing on Step One in this workbook about how you experience impaired self-esteem. (4) Read the following paragraphs.

As codependents, we experience either low or nonexistent self-esteem, or arrogance and grandiosity. As recovery begins, we have the sense of moving from whichever inappropriate level of esteem we experience toward the middle. At first this often feels like we're getting worse.

When moving from low self-esteem to healthy self-esteem, you may fear you're actually getting arrogant. When moving from arrogance and grandiosity to a more appropriate level of self-esteem, you may think you are losing power and getting worse by becoming weak and hopeless. At this point, you need to remind yourself that this movement is normal for recovery. You are making progress when you feel your level of self-worth either rising or dropping as you move toward healthy self-esteem. In fact, in the process of adjusting to what it feels like not to overvalue yourself, falsely empower yourself, and therefore offend other people, you will probably feel some pain. This pain is *not* the same as true low self-esteem, however, and you are probably not moving too far down the scale.

Following are exercises for each extreme of this core symptom: low or nonexistent self-esteem, and arrogance and grandiosity. Work on the section that best fits your experience of this symptom. Some people may need to work on both, since they swing back and forth.

TO RECOVER FROM LOW OR NONEXISTENT SELF-ESTEEM

WHAT TO DO This exercise has four parts. Read the explanations, then do the writing for each part. Remember, this is a process that takes time. Take as long as you need for each part.

MAKE A DECISION TO ESTEEM YOURSELF AND OTHERS

Building self-esteem from the low or nonexistent position begins with making a decision to value yourself and not consider yourself as being less valuable than anyone else. This decision expresses this truth: just as you are, you are enough. Just because you were born, you are precious. Your preciousness, or worth, is not up for debate. You were born an amazing creature filled with wonder and spiritual value. There is no question about whether you are or aren't of value in this sense. You are of equal value to everyone else.

As you've discovered earlier in this workbook, being out of touch with your own worth is due to the fact that when you were a child, important caregivers in your life did not esteem you in an appropriate way. In neglecting to do that, they were abusive whether they intended to be or not. It's not their "fault"; it's just a circumstance of your life.

But now as a mature adult, in recovery from the results of that abuse, you can make the decision to honor yourself and treat yourself as though you are precious. This is your absolute right and privilege as a human being.

When you make this decision to value yourself, you almost invariably start honoring other people as well. As you esteem yourself, you esteem other people. And this change can do wonderful things for your relationships.

Your self-esteem allows you to esteem others and to love the members of your family. And as you love you and that very abused, precious little child inside you, and quit punishing yourself with carried guilt and shame, you are more sensitive to your own children's being valuable, vulnerable, imperfect, needy and wanting, and immature. You are more able to respect those characteristics and stop trying to make them perfect. As a result, you can feel some worth without their having to be perfect children.

One way to affirm yourself is by learning to accept compliments from others. When you are experiencing low self-esteem, you probably have a painful reaction when told that you are wonderful. You probably avoid eye contact, turn red, can't talk, and can't accept what was said. At times you may cry because it hurts to take the compliment in. These behaviors indicate that you are having a shame attack, an inner sense of worthlessness, and you can't understand why anyone would say that you are wonderful.

Write in the following space in your own words a statement about your worth.

EXAMPLE	Just because I was born, I am enough. I can stop trying to earn my worth from my job, my children, and my family connections.

My Statement About My Decision to Value Myself

MAKE AN AFFIRMATION LIST

This second part of developing self-esteem is to make a list of affirmations.

Begin by thinking about a time when you were abused as a child, or made some mistake either as a child or as an adult that brought massive feelings of shame. Let yourself float back into that old shame-filled feeling reality. As you're feeling that carried shame that tells you you're no good, listen to all the adjectives and nouns you add to the statement "I am . . ." in your mind. For example, "I am worthless"; "I am bad"; "I am stupid"; "I am a lout"; "I am empty"; "I am awful"; "I am a slut"; "I am a creep"; "I am a jerk"; "I am a smelly person"; "I am inadequate"; whatever your particular set of statements is. Your statements may be very profane. Don't worry about that; many people's are. Continue until your mind surrenders all the negative adjectives and nouns that you tell yourself you are.

After your mind has become aware of what you tell yourself when you are less than perfect, write those negative statements in the column on the left in the following table. It is important to preface each statement with "I am" because shame is connected to your sense of who you are. Read the left column in the example before writing your own.

Then, opposite each negative noun or adjective you wrote about yourself, write a noun or adjective that will contradict it in an affirming way. Write these words down as a word exercise, whether you believe these things about yourself or not.

EXAMPLE

I am bad	I am good
I am inadequate	I am adequate
I am stupid	I am able to think well
I am empty	I am filled with value
I am awful	I am wonderful
I am worthless	I am a precious person
I am a lout	I am a nice person
I am a creep	I am an enjoyable person
I am a jerk	I am courteous and kind
I am a smelly person	I am clean and pleasant
I am a slut	I am appropriate in my sexual relationship

My Shame Messages	*My Positive Affirmations*
I am _____	I am _____
I am _____	I am _____
I am _____	I am _____
I am _____	I am _____
I am _____	I am _____
I am _____	I am _____
I am _____	I am _____
I am _____	I am _____
I am _____	I am _____
I am _____	I am _____
I am _____	I am _____
I am _____	I am _____
I am _____	I am _____

MAKE AN AFFIRMATION TAPE

When you have completed the list, cover up the left column so that you can no longer read it. Then get a blank cassette tape and a tape recorder. Record an opening sentence, then the positive affirmations list.

Write in the following space the introductory sentence you will record on your tape. Then make a note of the date your tape was recorded.

EXAMPLE

INTRODUCTORY SENTENCE:

I am Pia. The following is a list of affirmations that I use to dispute the carried shame core messages.

DATE RECORDED: August 23, 1984

INTRODUCTORY SENTENCE:

DATE RECORDED:

USE THE AFFIRMATION TAPE

After you've made your own tape, play it to yourself twice a day: in the morning when you get up and at night when you go to bed. This may seem too mechanical, but you may be amazed at the change in your feelings about yourself if you listen to the tape twice a day for a month.

As you begin to practice this exercise, more and more negative messages will usually become conscious. Now that the first list is out in the open, deeper shame messages or different ones or more adult ones may come up. These should also be written down with their refuting affirmations, and the new affirmations added to the tape. Eventually this deep hidden reservoir of shame messages will be drained and you will stop getting new ones. (The quantity of shame messages that comes up and the length of time it takes before you stop getting new ones indicate how deep your experiences of abuse are.)

I think our self-esteem and the way we think about ourselves has to do with our spirituality. So if you're in a Twelve-Step program using a daily affirmation book, I suggest that you read the book in the same period of time you listen to your tape. A book that has very positive material for codependents is *Daily Affirmations for Adult Children of Alcoholics* by Rokelle Lerner. Or you can use one of the other daily books that are recommended in various Twelve-Step programs. Read the book before you listen to the tape, listen to the tape, and then put them away.

Incorporating this affirmation tape with things you do to develop your spiritual life makes the exercise a lot easier, and the self-esteem seems to come faster.

Make a note of the dates you play your tape to yourself.

DATES PLAYED:			

Go to page 313 to continue writing about your recovery (Tracking Progress).

To Recover From Arrogance and Grandiosity

WHAT TO DO   This exercise has two parts. Read the explanation, then do the writing for each part. Remember, this is a process that takes time. Take as long as you need for each part.

MAKE A DECISION TO ESTEEM OTHERS EQUALLY TO YOURSELF

The first step in recovering from the extreme of arrogance and grandiosity is understanding and accepting that arrogance and grandiosity are dysfunctional and abusive to other people. In recovery it is helpful to begin by making a decision to esteem others as equal to yourself.

Write in the following space in your own words a statement about your worth.

EXAMPLE

> I am a perfectly imperfect person and do not have the right to view myself as better than anyone else.

My Statement About My Decision to Esteem Others Equally to Myself

The position of arrogance and grandiosity often comes from comparing yourself to others and coming up better than that other person. Recovery involves stopping this form of judging and comparing except in the important values relating to murder, rape, incest, physical violence, war, and so on. You must discipline your mind by refuting the judging messages with messages about other people having equal value with yourself.

In the column on the left, write down specific instances in which you compare yourself with someone and judge yourself superior to that person. Then, in the column on the right, write out a healthy statement about the equality of your value and the value of the other person.

EXAMPLE	JUDGMENTS I HAVE MADE ABOUT MY SUPERIORITY TO OTHERS	HEALTHY ATTITUDES ABOUT MY VALUE AND THAT OF OTHERS
	I am better than Julie because her house smells like dirty cat litter.	Julie has as much value as I do even if she chooses to tolerate the smell of cat litter.
	I am better than Mr. S. because he got a speeding ticket.	Mr. S. has as much value as I do even if he gets a speeding ticket
	I am better than Sammy because he is retarded and does embarrassing things in public.	Sammy has as much value as I do even when his behavior is different than that of most people because of being retarded.

JUDGMENTS I HAVE MADE ABOUT MY SUPERIORITY TO OTHERS	HEALTHY ATTITUDES ABOUT MY VALUE AND THAT OF OTHERS

Many times, when you stop judging yourself to be superior, you move to feelings of being less than others. If this happens to you, work on the previous exercises regarding how to counteract the shame messages you now experience.

TRACKING PROGRESS

As you make progress with this symptom, you will notice how you are more able to experience your own worth from within, putting yourself neither less than nor better than others, regaining the mature adult characteristics described in chapter 4 of *Facing Codependence.* Improvement means that as you encounter others, you look at yourself as of equal value to them or you look at them as of equal value to you.

WHAT TO DO

Describe in the following space incidents in which you notice an improvement: Become aware of feelings you may experience, such as pain or fear, and note them also.

Signs of Improvement in My Self-Esteem

NAME: **DATE:**

WHAT HAPPENED:

FEELINGS NOTED:

NAME: **DATE:**

WHAT HAPPENED:

FEELINGS NOTED:

NAME: **DATE:**

WHAT HAPPENED:

FEELINGS NOTED:

NAME: **DATE:**

WHAT HAPPENED:

FEELINGS NOTED:

Setting External Boundaries

After improving your self-esteem, the next component of recovery is to devise healthy boundaries, both to protect yourself from others and to keep yourself from authentically offending others. Our boundary system has two subsystems: external and internal. Our external boundary system protects us physically and sexually and helps us keep an appropriate physical distance from others and respect the sexual boundaries of others. The internal boundary is related to thinking, feeling, and behaving and will be discussed in the next section.

PURPOSE OF EXERCISES

You did the first exercise toward establishing your boundaries when you evaluated the condition of each part of your boundary system in your written Step One. Now you can begin to correct the dysfunctional aspects of your boundaries by doing the following exercises.

BACKGROUND READING

(1) Review pages 11–21 of *Facing Codependence,* about boundary impairment and healthy boundaries. (2) Review pages 80–82 of *Facing Codependence,* about a child's vulnerability in a dysfunctional family. (3) Review your own writing in Step One in this workbook about the condition of your external boundaries. (4) Read the following material.

Boundary recovery begins when you acknowledge and accept these three statements:

1. Nobody has the right to touch you (an adult) without your permission. Also, nobody has the right to be sexual with you without your permission.

2. People who have your permission to touch you may touch you only in the way in which you want to be touched. Also, people with whom you have agreed to be sexual may only be sexual with you in the ways you agree to.

3. It's your responsibility to take control over how, when, where, and who touches you, and with whom, when, and how you will be sexual.

You are in recovery when you exercise those controls with most people, except a major offender.

DETERMINING WHERE YOUR EXTERNAL BOUNDARY IS

Begin to develop your awareness of when other people are too close to you. Take note of your discomfort when people stand or move too close to you. This will make you more aware that you need to take care of yourself. I have used two methods to help me become mindful of my own requirement for physical distance from others:

1. Stand across a room from someone and make eye contact with him or her. Walk slowly toward the person and stop when you start feeling uncomfortable, then back up and stand where you feel comfortable. The distance between you and the other person shows how large your external boundary is. The amount of physical distance you need varies as you approach different people, depending on many factors, such as how well you know the other person, how you're responding to that person at the time, and so on.

2. Another simple gauge of a comfortable distance between you and someone else is to look that person in the eye. If it is difficult or you can't, the person is probably too close to you.

The amount of distance you need from another person can be different on various occasions with the *same* person. For instance, if my husband Pat and I are getting along and I feel good about our relationship, he can stand close to me and I'm very comfortable. If, however, he's angry with me or I'm angry with him, we don't stand so close. If we're extremely angry, we may actually stand eighteen feet away from each other in the living room to talk.

Also, the distance you need varies from person to person. You can allow people who feel "safe" to get closer to you. You require more distance from other people who feel more threatening for whatever reason. As you develop boundaries, you will be able to back away from such people and negotiate the distance between you, not letting them stand too close to you any longer.

WHAT TO DO

Ask two or three safe people (such as members of your Codependents Anonymous group, a sponsor, a spouse) to try the physical boundary test with you.

1. Ask each person for permission to walk toward him or her until you feel the energy resistance of your own boundary.

2. Stop walking and note the distance.

3. Try to look him or her in the eye at that distance. If you need to adjust in order to make eye contact, do so and note the new distance.

4. Ask that person if your boundary distance feels comfortable to him or her. If not, ask how he or she would adjust it. Note the person's preference, while still keeping in mind that your need for space is your own and will often be different from that of other people. It is functional for the person needing the most space to be given that space by the other person.

Record in the following space what happened.

My Experiments with Physical Boundaries

1. **NAME OF PERSON:**

   Amt. of space needed for boundary that day:

   Did I readjust after making eye contact?

   Was the other person's boundary different?

   Other comments:

2. **NAME OF PERSON:**

   Amt. of space needed for boundary that day:

   Did I readjust after making eye contact?

   Was the other person's boundary different?

   Other comments:

3. **NAME OF PERSON:**

   Amt. of space needed for boundary that day:

   Did I readjust after making eye contact?

   Was the other person's boundary different?

   Other comments:

VISUALIZING YOUR EXTERNAL BOUNDARY

You can strengthen your external boundary by visualizing it in concrete form. While the visualizing can be done in many ways, here is a way I find helpful. Close your eyes and imagine a jar made of a sturdy but expandable material. In your mind, enlarge this jar until it is big enough to fit over you. This jar represents your external boundary. It is not appropriate ever to let anyone inside your boundary. Practice expanding your boundary to get distance and then pulling it in close to you to receive a hug or to be sexual. With this boundary in place in your mind, proceed as follows.

THE PHYSICAL BOUNDARY

Set your physical external boundary by memorizing and saying this statement to yourself:

> I have the right to determine who touches me, when, where, and how that person touches me, and how close to me I allow a person to stand, and vice versa.

With this statement, you claim ownership of your body and acknowledge that nobody has the right to stand too close to you or touch you without your permission. On the other hand, as you give yourself the right to have a self-determined boundary, you also give other people the right to determine how close you can get and whether you can touch them. Each of us has the right to negotiate that space or distance.

For example, if you're uncomfortable because somebody is standing too close, you might say to the person, "You're standing too close. Would you please move back?" Perhaps someone you don't know walks up and puts his arm around you. His action is not sexual, but he is just too close physically for your comfort. You have the right to turn and say graciously, "I don't know you well enough for you to put your arm around me, and I'm uncomfortable. Would you please take your arm down and step back?" You can't stop him from touching you if you don't see him coming. But you can set your boundary as soon as you feel uncomfortable.

I do this for myself with strangers, with friends, with my husband, and with my kids. And I allow them to do this with me, too.

It's imperative for legitimate peace and security to be able to set boundaries. Yet people who have been physically abused often have a lot of difficulty asking others to move or saying no to anyone who gets too close to them for comfort. They think they are being rude or that they don't have the right to tell someone not to touch them. But this fear and reticence is part of the disease of codependence. *Every* adult has the right to determine what is done to his or her own body. Everyone has the right and the duty to set boundaries when relating to other people.

THE SEXUAL BOUNDARY

Just as you did for your physical boundary, visualize your sexual boundary as an inverted jar. Then set your sexual boundary by memorizing and saying this statement to yourself:

> I have the right to determine with whom, where, when, and how I will be sexual, and vice versa.

That means that nobody has the right to tell you that you have to be sexual with him or her, nor tell you how, when, or where you will be sexual. You alone determine that. You need only face the consequences of your choices. On the other hand, as you determine that boundary for yourself, you also give any other person you might relate to sexually the right to make that determination for himself or herself. So if you're trying to negotiate being sexual with your spouse, who says, "No, thank you," that's the end of it. He or she has the right to tell you, "No, I don't want to be sexual with you now." Or he or she might need to say, "Yes, I want to be sexual, but I don't want to do it that way." This boundary allows you to be sexually protected and also to act appropriately with others.

Your sexual boundary determines not only whether or not you will be sexual, but also *in what way* you will be sexual. For example, Irene might want to be sexual with her husband Jim, but not in a particular way that Jim wants to (for example, her breasts hurt and she doesn't want him to touch them). So how does she set her boundary to exclude a specific kind of sexual behavior with which she is not comfortable, without excluding all sexual behavior with her husband?

First, she says, "I'll be sexual with you but my breasts are sore tonight, so please be careful about touching them." She has her imaginary jar (sexual boundary) pulled in close as if glued to her to allow Jim close to her body, but when the boundary comes to her breasts she imagines the boundary bubbling out there.

WHAT TO DO

Use the following to write about instances when you have noticed that someone has crossed your physical or sexual boundary. Describe the situation and what you did and/or said (if anything) to protect yourself.

EXAMPLE

> I was standing in line at the grocery store when I felt the hair on the back of my neck stand up. I turned and realized the woman behind me was only inches from me. She had her back to me and was scanning the magazine rack. I couldn't move forward because I'd bump my grocery cart into the person ahead of me in line. So I said to her, "Excuse me, but I'm uncomfortable with you standing so close. Could you move back, please?" I gave her a great big smile. She was glad to move back and did. I never knew how much having people too close bothered me or that I could do anything about it before!

Times When Someone Has Crossed My External Boundaries

Use the following space to record instances when you have realized or been told you were invading someone else's physical or sexual boundary. Name the person and describe the situation and what the other person did or said to let you know, and also your response.

EXAMPLE

I was talking to a girl I knew at a party and I suddenly noticed she kept stepping back from me. I'd move up and then she'd step back again. I also noticed that she wasn't looking at me when I talked or when she answered. It occurred to me that maybe I was crowding her a little bit. I said, "Hey, am I standing too close to you?" and I moved back. She said, "Yes, I guess you were," and shrugged, but we went on talking and I no longer had the impression she was trying to get away from me. She looked me in the eye and smiled and talked to me for a long time. I guess I've been standing too close to people for years and didn't realize it.

Times When I Have Crossed Someone's External Boundaries

TRACKING IMPROVEMENT

As you recover regarding this symptom, you will notice that you are better able to negotiate distance and touch with others, physically and sexually. You may feel less vulnerable (able to say no), less antidependent (able to ask for physical or sexual nurturing), or less needless/wantless (more able to recognize that you need physical space, physical affection, more sex, less sex, or different kinds of sexual behaviors), and more able to express your feelings about your needs and wants.

WHAT TO DO

Describe in the following space any incidents that seem like examples of recovery regarding setting external boundaries.

Signs of Improvement of My External Boundaries

DATE:
WHAT HAPPENED:

DATE:
WHAT HAPPENED:

Setting Internal Boundaries

You need an internal boundary so you can detach enough to accurately hear what another person tells you about who he or she is, and so you can separate that person's feelings and thoughts from your own. With a good internal boundary, you can be in a relationship without projecting your own skewed interpretations onto the other person or allowing that person's fear or pain, for instance, to *become your own* and overwhelm you. And an intact internal boundary is especially helpful and necessary when someone is confronting you.

With a healthy internal boundary, you can truly detach from other people while staying in caring relationships. You can begin to choose your own behavior, thinking, and feeling reality rather than making strong automatic responses that baffle you. Therefore, learning to set an internal boundary is a very big part of recovery from codependence. Learning to set a healthy internal boundary usually takes more time, practice, and patience than setting an external boundary because it's not something you can touch or feel.

PURPOSE OF EXERCISES

These exercises are to help you learn to recognize when someone has authentically transgressed your internal boundary, and when you have transgressed someone else's internal boundary, and to help you develop your own healthy internal boundary system.

BACKGROUND READING

Before doing the following exercises, read (1) your own writing in Step One of this workbook about your internal boundaries and (2) the following paragraphs.

When your codependence is operating, you blame other people for your thoughts, feelings, and behavior, and blame yourself for other people's thoughts, feelings, and behavior. You have the idea that other people *make* you think, feel, or do things, or push your buttons.

"If you just wouldn't look at her that way I wouldn't feel jealous!" "If you'd just come home at night when I want you to, I wouldn't be so upset and worried." "If you'd be nicer to me, I wouldn't have to overeat and I could lose weight." "I can't tell her I'm angry about what she said about me, because that would make her cry and ruin the weekend." This is *erroneous, dysfunctional thinking*.

Nobody pushes your buttons. Nobody "makes" you angry, and nobody really can "hurt your feelings," *unless* he or she is committing a genuine act of offense. When you observe something happening, that event first enters your mind as *thoughts* about the event that give the event meaning. And it is that *meaning* your mind gives the event that triggers your *feeling* reality—not the event itself. As a result of that self-generated feeling reality, you choose your behavior. So you are responsible for your own thinking, feeling, and what you do or don't do. The process works like this:

EVENTS ➡ THOUGHTS ➡ MEANING CHOICE ➡ FEELINGS ➡ BEHAVIOR

Since the experience of abuse in your past leads to skewed thinking about present events, you may often come up with some distorted meanings for perfectly nonoffensive events. As my husband has said to me more than once, "Pia, you can take perfectly good data into your head, and by the time you finish giving it meaning, it has very little to do with reality."

By the same token, you don't have the power to cause anybody else to think, feel, or do or not do anything. When you say or do something, the other person takes it in, gives it meaning, and has feelings and behaviors about it, all on his or her own. This is why some people can stay calm and serene when being criticized and other people dissolve into tears when someone doesn't smile at them.

The skewed thinking process often begins in childhood when the parent blames the child for the abuse the parent is doing. And being abused creates other kinds of skewed thinking. Since thinking triggers feelings, skewed thinking makes it hard for codependents to know what they are really feeling or what is really happening in their relationships.

I am convinced that to recover, a codependent must grasp this phenomenon of skewed thinking and how this is responsible for many of the codependent's painful feelings and mistakes in behavioral responses. But becoming aware of this skewed thinking process is very difficult, since it is your mind (which thinks in a skewed way) that must learn to recognize the skewed process and how it is affecting your feelings. This factor makes recovery from codependence more complex. But with acceptance of the fact that your thinking is very likely to be skewed, it is not impossible.

Another painful consequence of lack of healthy internal boundaries is that when someone is telling you his or her thoughts and opinions, you think you must either agree with the person, giving up your own thinking reality, or you must argue with the person until your opinion wins. This damages and bruises relationships a great deal. But these are not the only choices. A person with good internal boundaries does not have to *convince others* of the validity of his or her reality.

It is important to acknowledge and accept the following as you begin to work on improving your internal boundaries:

Thoughts: You have the right to think what you think; you only need to face the consequences of your thinking.

Feelings: You have the right to whatever feelings you have. You just need to be careful that you don't offend someone with your feelings by expressing them immoderately. Your feelings are based on your thinking, and you can't change them except by changing your thinking.

Behavior: You have the right to do or not do whatever you need to for yourself. You have the right to determine what your behavior needs to be for yourself. You need only note the impact of your behavior on other people and be willing to face the consequences. If your behavior is authentically offensive to another person, you are responsible for the impact of it.

To set your internal boundary, you must begin acting and thinking as if you *do in fact* have the right to think, feel, and do whatever you want to think, feel, and do. Hearing other people describe this process in Twelve-Step meetings or watching sponsors or friends actually do it in their own lives can add much courage and motivation to begin living this way yourself.

At the same time, you must be aware that while you have the right to think what you think, the way your thinking affects your emotional reality and your behavior bears examining. Your skewed thinking creates painful and sometimes unnecessary codependent feeling reality. You need strong internal boundaries within which to examine your thinking, get more information, and correct any thinking you find to be skewed. Healthy thinking in recovery can relieve some of the painful emotional reactions you have been subject to when operating in codependence.

MAKING YOUR INTERNAL BOUNDARY WORK

Keep in mind that when you first start to consciously set an internal boundary it will probably feel very strange and you may not be very successful at it. I've noticed that most codependents have to attempt the process many times before it works for them. But keep working with this anyway, because the first time it works for you, I believe you will be amazed at how wonderful you feel.

The following exercise has helped me and others learn how to make the internal boundary work.

Whenever someone confronts you by telling you his or her thinking and feeling reality about you, use the following steps to set your internal boundary:

1. Imagine your external boundary in a form such as an inverted jar over you or an energy force field surrounding you that you can see in your mind.

2. Hold your ear lobe between your thumb and forefinger and incline your head slightly toward the person to whom you're listening, to remind yourself that the functional thing to do at the moment is to listen, not defend yourself. (I started doing this because whenever my husband confronted me I used to have a shame attack or rage attack instantly, and I didn't hear a thing he said.)

3. Imagine your internal boundary in a form such as a bulletproof vest or a hard metal plate under your skin on your chest. The image I use of my internal boundary has little doors in it that open to the inside. Only I control when they open. They cannot be opened from the outside.

4. Silently repeat to yourself this memorized statement about the other person:

   What you think, feel, and choose to do or not do at this moment is more about you and your history than it is about what I have said or done (and vice versa), unless I have committed an authentic act of offense.

5. Listen to hear if the information coming to you is true, not true, or questionable, and then take the appropriate action.

THE PROCESS IN ACTION

Harry comes in to the kitchen and says to his wife Anne, "I need to tell you that I'm angry with you." Right then she knows a confrontation is happening. He's going to express his thinking and feeling reality to her. Anne must set her internal boundary so she can hear what Harry has to say and be intimate and appropriate.

First, Anne imagines her external boundary and imagines setting it down over her whole body. Next, she reminds herself that she is to be listening to Harry, not defending herself. She might even hold or touch her ear lobe as a reminder. Then Anne sets her internal boundary by imagining a sheet of metal under the skin on her chest, doors facing in. She says to herself: "What Harry thinks, feels, and chooses to do or not do at this moment is more about Harry's history than it is about what I have said or done, unless I have authentically offended him." That helps Anne to be able to hear Harry and then note the impact of her behavior on him. As she notes the impact of her behavior on him, she must remember that the *impact* is still more about him than it is about her, unless she has transgressed one of Harry's boundaries. If Harry is just experiencing Anne's reality and not liking it, his sensibilities may feel "offended." But I am not using the term "offended" in this way.

Anne listens to what Harry says, using her internal boundary. She reminds herself, "I have the right to determine whether what Harry is saying about me is true, not true, or questionable." After he has finished, she determines for herself which of the three it is.

True: It did happen as he's describing it.

Not true: It did not happen as he is describing it.

Questionable: Anne isn't sure whether it happened or not.

If she decides the information is true, even if it is threatening to her self-concept, she then imagines it as a little piece of matter out in front of her, lets it come through the external boundary and the door in her internal boundary, and has her feelings about it. It may feel painful or wonderful, depending on what Harry is confronting her about.

Let's say, for example, that Anne forgot to pick Harry up at work as she'd promised to do, and as a result he missed a golf game with his boss. She realizes it is true, lets the information in through her external and internal boundaries, feels the guilt, and decides how she will make amends.

This is what I mean when I say that to recover, you must "hug your demons or they'll bite you in the ass." Letting the truth come through our external and internal boundaries and acknowledging it is "hugging your demons." It is a mature act, and is also what I mean by being accountable.

After Anne owns her feelings about the true material from Harry, she can take any appropriate action she may wish to about what he has told her. She can thank him, make amends, or do what she considers to be mature for her about the information Harry has shared.

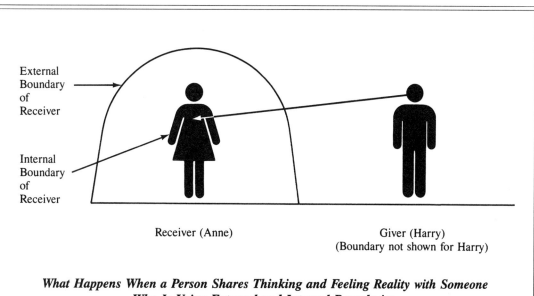

External
Boundary
of
Receiver

Internal
Boundary
of
Receiver

Receiver (Anne)

Giver (Harry)
(Boundary not shown for Harry)

***What Happens When a Person Shares Thinking and Feeling Reality with Someone
Who Is Using External and Internal Boundaries.
When the information is* true, *receiver lets it through her external and internal boundaries.***

If Anne listens and decides that the information is *not* true, she imagines that the little lump of information hits her external boundary and bounces to the floor. She acknowledges to Harry that she heard him, by some means such as nodding her head. She may even express some feelings about the fact that Harry is having a painful experience by saying something like "That sounds painful." But it is not necessary for her to take responsibility for what he is feeling, thinking, or doing or not doing. In fact, it is an act of maturity *not* to take responsibility for something when she has not committed any authentically offensive act. A mature person is able to tolerate the fact that somebody has a different sense of reality about what happened, and doesn't have to argue, justify himself or herself, or prevail. With maturity, Anne can let Harry (or anyone else) have whatever his reality is.

Remember that much of Harry's reality is related to his own history. And only if Anne has authentically offended him is it helpful to her to let that confrontive information inside her boundaries and to have feelings about it.

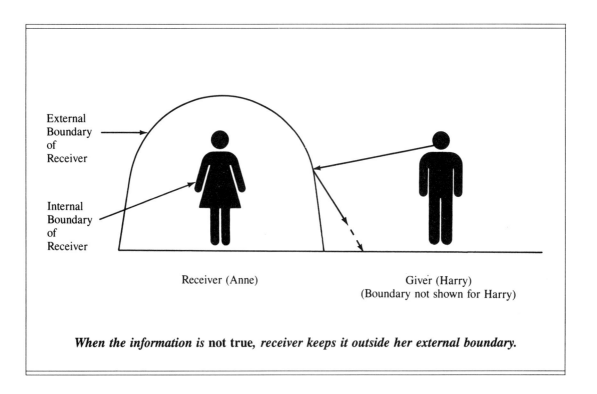

External
Boundary
of
Receiver

Internal
Boundary
of
Receiver

Receiver (Anne)

Giver (Harry)
(Boundary not shown for Harry)

*When the information is **not** true, receiver keeps it outside her external boundary.*

For most codependents who set out to develop an internal boundary system, most information falls in the questionable category. So if you find that you are often in doubt about the truth of a confrontive claim, don't think there is something strange about you. That is very common. With practice and recovery you will recognize more easily what is true about yourself and what isn't. But there is a way to deal with questionable confrontive material.

If Anne decides Harry's confrontive information is questionable, she lets that little piece of information go through her external boundary, brings it around behind her, and puts it on her shoulder where she can watch it . . . but she allows nothing to enter her internal boundary. Eventually, when she gets enough data about the information Harry has given her, Anne will very likely have a definite sense of whether the statement is either not true or true. If the information turns out to be not true, then she throws it outside her external boundary. If she realizes it is true, she lets it in through a door in her internal boundary and has her feelings about it. That, too, takes maturity. This latter scenario of handling questionable information is the experience most people have in treatment when their families confront them.

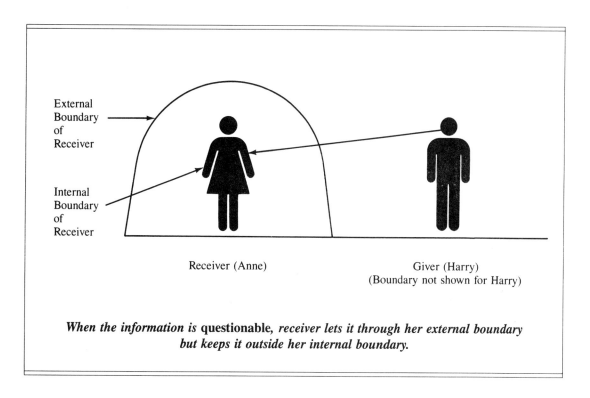

External
Boundary
of
Receiver

Internal
Boundary
of
Receiver

Receiver (Anne)

Giver (Harry)
(Boundary not shown for Harry)

When the information is **questionable,** *receiver lets it through her external boundary but keeps it outside her internal boundary.*

WHAT ABOUT DISPUTING UNTRUE STATEMENTS?

Many people ask me, "If the confrontive material is not true, can't I dispute what the person is confronting me with?" I recommend not to argue or dispute untrue statements at first, but to practice the process as I have described it. By practicing keeping your mouth shut, you gradually become more comfortable when other people disagree with you or don't have the same sense about you that you have. This allows the other person to be who he or she is and teaches you to accept the fact that not everyone sees you the way you do. And this way of handling confrontive situations is much more serene for those codependents who have always hated confrontations.

This process may be difficult to practice at first because a real issue for many codependents is *control*. We want to make sure that everybody believes what we believe and that what's happening is in accordance with what we believe. But this is an impossible stance, since all people will never have the same perceptions about us (or anything else) that we do. *Insisting that others agree with our perceptions destroys or bruises relationships.*

Learning to communicate by practicing this exercise can allow you to live in mature action for yourself rather than in constant codependent reaction to other people.

If you're on Harry's end of the experience and are confronting someone, understand that you have the right to confront anybody with your reality and need only face the consequences of doing so. But before you confront someone with your reality, it is helpful to remind yourself that your reality is more about you than the person you're confronting, unless that person has authentically offended you. You may find as time goes on that more and more frequently you check your own thinking that sets up your confrontive feelings and discover that the "offense" you attributed to the other person is about your interpretation. If you check that out with the other person, you may have a much more successful time communicating intimately and finding the truth about what really happened.

TWO IMPORTANT CAVEATS

Two extemely important caveats must be considered along with the information about a functional internal boundary. The first one is: although you know that you are not responsible for how someone else is responding to you, if you're in a relationship you *are* responsible for noting the impact of your behavior on the other person. When you note the impact, you may feel some pain at seeing the person you care for in pain, even though your behavior has not been authentically offensive. *But with healthy internal boundaries you do not feel guilt or shame, or feel responsible for causing the pain.* Noting the impact of your behavior on others is extremely important to having healthy relationships.

If you are not noting the impact of your behavior on the other person, you can't adjust your reality in the interest of making the relationship more comfortable. The attitude of "Tough! Your pain is your problem. I don't care," will *not* lead to recovery and the growth of intimacy.

For example, say I move something that belongs to my husband (that I have the right to move). My husband reacts to the fact that I moved it. I know, when my boundary is standing up well, that his reaction to whatever I have done is more about him and his history than what I've said or done, as long as I haven't offended him.

But I am in a relationship with him and I love and care about him. It's important to note the impact of my behavior, because I may want to adjust some of it so we can live together more comfortably, even though I know his reaction to my behavior is about his history, not because I am being offensive in any way.

With my internal boundary working, I don't have feelings of shame and guilt about offending him, but I do learn about him and his feelings about the issue in question, and perhaps, if the issue is serious enough for him, feel some pain about seeing my loved one in pain. Then I can decide whether I want to adjust my behavior to make our relationship more comfortable. As long as I do not *have* to adjust so much that I lose touch with myself or cannot express my own reality comfortably, such adjustments are fine.

The other caveat is: if one person in an exchange has authentically offended the other by pushing through his or her boundary system, and has physically, sexually, intellectually, emotionally, or spiritually attacked the other person, then the offender *cannot* truly say that the victim's reaction is about the *victim's history*. That statement does not hold in the victim-offender situation.

For example, let's say that one person has touched another without permission, or has screamed at or ridiculed the other person's intellectual ability, all of which are authentic offensive acts. In this instance, the person who did the offensive act is liable for the effect on the other person. In other words, I can't slap my husband in anger (or for any reason) and then, when he responds with a lot of anger and pain, say to him, "That's more about you and your history than about my slapping you across the face." That's *not* the case.

WHAT TO DO

Use the following space to record instances when someone has confronted you by telling you his or her thinking and feelings about some part of your reality (such as your behavior or your thinking). Were you able to establish an external and internal boundary and listen, deciding if the information were true, not true, or questionable? Name the person, describe what he or she confronted you with, and describe how you used internal boundaries (if at all) to have a more functional reaction.

EXAMPLE

My mother told me in a letter that she was angry and felt rejected by my decision not to come home during the holidays. My decision was based on my true preference to go with my boyfriend to his father's ranch, not as a rejection of mother. I realized that her anger and belief that she was being rejected was more about her and her history than about my decision, so I noted the impact of my behavior on her but didn't feel guilt or responsibility.

Or, if your first attempt at having internal boundaries isn't so successful:

EXAMPLE

> I knew it wasn't true, that I wasn't rejecting her, but I blamed myself for rejecting her and suffered for a while before I realized what I was doing.

Times When I Have Used Internal Boundaries When Confronted

1. **DATE:**
   WHAT HAPPENED:

2. **DATE:**
   WHAT HAPPENED:

3. **DATE:**
   WHAT HAPPENED:

4. DATE:
   WHAT HAPPENED:

5. DATE:
   WHAT HAPPENED:

6. DATE:
   WHAT HAPPENED:

Use the following space to write about instances when you have decided to confront someone with your thinking and feelings about something the person has said or done. Were you able to do so in a nonblaming way, remembering that your thinking and feelings are more about you and your history than about the other person? Name the person, describe the content of your confrontation, and how you presented it.

EXAMPLE

I made arrangements to have my collie groomed because he was matted and dirty. I asked my husband to pick up the dog at the groomer's because I would be unable to do so. When I asked him to pick up the dog he told me he thought it was unnecessary to have the dog groomed. I felt annoyed when he said that. When I got home I stated to him, "When you said it was unnecessary to get the dog groomed, I felt mildly angry."

Times When I Have Confronted Others

1. **DATE:**
   WHAT HAPPENED:

2. **DATE:**
   WHAT HAPPENED:

3. **DATE:**
   WHAT HAPPENED:

4. **DATE:**

   WHAT HAPPENED:

5. **DATE:**

   WHAT HAPPENED:

6. **DATE:**

   WHAT HAPPENED:

Use the following space to record instances when you have had the opportunity to decide whether to share your opinion (thinking reality) with someone. What was the issue? How did you use internal boundaries (if at all) to help you if you were able to own your own opinion? If you did not acknowledge your thinking, describe the process that prevented you from doing so.

EXAMPLE

The discussion at the party turned to the new dean of the university. Most people seemed to be critical of him. Our neighbor, Dan, said he didn't like the man and was sorry he'd gotten the position. But I had met the new dean at church the week before and thought he seemed to be an intelligent, caring individual who would be good for the university. In my opinion, the press had made biased insinuations about him in the paper, not giving him a fair chance before making judgments. There was a lull in the conversation, and I managed to say, "Dean Rutherford was at our church last Sunday." People looked at me and I thought, "I could just stop there and not tell them what I thought about him and the press. But these are my friends. After all, I have the right to think what I think. I'll see what happens." Then I imagined my bulletproof vest and told them what I thought about the dean and the press. The discussion continued, Dan laughed and looked "superior," but I told myself that was about Dan and his history. Then Mary said she had thought the same thing I did about the press. I felt wonderful!

Times When I Have Shared or Chosen Not to Share My Thinking Reality

1. **DATE:**
   WHAT HAPPENED:

2. **DATE:**
   WHAT HAPPENED:

3. **DATE:**
   WHAT HAPPENED:

4. DATE:
WHAT HAPPENED:

5. DATE:
WHAT HAPPENED:

6. DATE:
WHAT HAPPENED:

Use the following space to record instances when someone else has shared thinking reality with you that you did not agree with. What was the issue? How did you use internal boundaries to help you simply listen to that person's thinking, if you were able to do this? Were you swayed to change your thinking and agree with him or her? Were you "compelled" to argue with him or her in an attempt to get his or her agreement with your thinking?

EXAMPLE	

I am on the board of an organization that provides for under-privileged families in my town. Last Thursday, George, knowing this, told me that he thought people were taking advantage of the organization, getting free food when they really had the money to buy food. That's why he didn't support it. I knew that we had guidelines and procedures for keeping a check on this, and that George's father had been vehemently against welfare of any kind. Instead of arguing with George, I simply smiled and sincerely said, "Oh, really? That's an interesting thought," and let it go. I said to myself, George's opinion is more about him and his history than about what I'm doing through that organization. Saying that helped me keep from feeling anger and from arguing with him and justifying our guidelines and procedures. I walked away and forgot about it until right now when I read this question. It hasn't bothered me a bit!

How I Have Reacted When Someone Has Shared Thinking with Which I Haven't Agreed

1. **DATE:**
   WHAT HAPPENED:

2. **DATE:**
   WHAT HAPPENED:

3. **DATE:**
   WHAT HAPPENED:

4. **DATE:**
   WHAT HAPPENED:

5. **DATE:**
   WHAT HAPPENED:

6. **DATE:**
   WHAT HAPPENED:

Use the following space to record instances when someone has shared his or her feeling reality with you. How did you use internal boundaries to help you simply listen to that person's reality, if you were able to do this? Were you swayed to say something to lessen or change that person's feelings?

EXAMPLE

I went to lunch with Elsie, whose daughter has decided to drop out of college to marry a young man who has no job and, in Elsie's opinion, little prospect of getting one. Elsie told me through her tears how upset she is about this, how her hopes and dreams for her daughter have been ruined. She felt depressed, angry, and afraid for her daughter and said she was sure that the marriage would never last. I imagined my bulletproof vest and told myself that Elsie has the right to think and feel what she thinks and feels and I do not have the right to try to change that. I kept thinking of all the things I've learned about detachment to tell her about, but didn't find a way to share my own experience because Elsie talked nonstop. I ended up telling her I thought it sounded like a difficult time for her. After lunch I felt kind of down, but then I reminded myself that those things were not happening to me or my daughter and that I had a right to feel and think about my own life, whatever my friends were feeling about theirs. So I didn't go into a depression over Elsie's daughter's problems, or start obsessing about how to save Elsie from her pain. I went on with my plans for a dinner party this weekend and had a great day.

How I Have Reacted When Someone Has Shared Feelings with Me

1. DATE:
   WHAT HAPPENED:

2. DATE:
   WHAT HAPPENED:

3. DATE:
   WHAT HAPPENED:

4. DATE

   WHAT HAPPENED:

5. DATE:

   WHAT HAPPENED:

6. DATE:

   WHAT HAPPENED:

TRACKING IMPROVEMENT

As recovery progresses, you will notice that you are more comfortable internally when others share their thinking and feeling reality with you. If you have been without boundaries, you will be more able to control how much vulnerability you have. Your own feelings and thinking will be going on while you listen to others—a sense of a separate self will begin to emerge. If you have used walls of anger or fear in the past, you will begin to feel more calm and confident (less invulnerable), able to share your reality with others and hear theirs without inappropriate anger or fear.

WHAT TO DO

Describe any incidents when you become aware of progress in using appropriate internal boundaries.

EXAMPLE

> My husband shared with me that he thought my son should go to an in-state public university instead of a private, out-of-state school because the difference in the quality of education is minimal and the cost difference is large. As he said this, I felt mild pain and some irritation. In the past I know I would have felt shame and guilt and would have also gone on to agree with him, even though originally I agreed with my son's decision to go out of state. As I listened to my husband, I said to myself, "He has a right to his opinion, and I have a right to mine. I disagree with him and am going to support my son's decision." I then told my husband, "I hear you. However, I support my son in what he is doing." I felt centered and in control of myself. I saw my husband look irritated and did not say anything more.

Signs of Improvement of My Internal Boundaries

Owning Your Own Reality

The bottom-line question for most codependents is: Who am I? Recovery with regard to the symptom of difficulty owning your own reality is the key to answering this question. When you sense your reality, you know better who you are.

The first two symptoms of codependence contribute to the difficulty with recognizing, acknowledging, and accepting your own reality. To review, they are (1) that you could not experience self-esteem at the appropriate level (feeling you were either less than or better than others) and (2) that you could not set appropriate external or internal boundaries for yourself, leaving you without the protection you need to own your reality. After you have worked on these two preceding core symptoms, you can turn to this vital area of recovery.

PURPOSE OF EXERCISES

These exercises are designed to help you (1) improve your ability to own your own physical reality (appearance and bodily functioning), thinking, feelings, and behavior, and (2) improve your level of comfort with your own imperfection.

BACKGROUND READING

(1) Review pages 21–28 of *Facing Codependence*, about the symptom of difficulty owning your reality. (2) Review pages 82–85 of *Facing Codependence*, about a child's imperfection in a dysfunctional family. (3) Review the writing you did in Step One in this workbook about the way you experience this symptom in your own life. (4) Read the following paragraphs.

As described in chapters 2 and 5 of *Facing Codependence*, difficulty owning our reality stems from not having our own childhood imperfection accepted, understood, and guided by our major caregivers. As a result, we responded in one of two ways: (1) we became a rebellious, "bad" person who doesn't try to do anything well at all because it was so impossible during childhood to meet our caregivers' perceived demands for perfection (we learned a "Why bother?" attitude for life), or (2) we expended a vast amount of energy trying to be perfectly correct and appropriate (according to the desires of our caregivers) in our physical appearance, our thinking, our emotions, and our behavior because we thought that by being perfect we could then avoid the pain of being attacked, shamed, punished, and/or ignored when we presented our own reality to our caregivers. We succeeded to various degrees but paid an enormous personal price. The attitude is "If I'm perfect enough I can avoid a lot of pain, shame, fear, and so on. When people are angry with me about my mistakes, it is my fault for not being perfect."

The exercises are divided into three parts. In the first part, you will examine your ability to own your shortcomings and imperfections. In the second part, you will reassess your ability to own the four parts of reality. And the third part deals specifically with each area of reality: the body, thinking, feelings, and behavior.

CHANGES IN OWNING YOUR IMPERFECTION

WHAT TO DO Use the following space to write about changes you have noticed in the rebellious/"bad" or perfect/"good" stance toward life you adopted during childhood.

EXAMPLE

My childhood stance in life was perfect/"good." I used to not even consider that I might be wrong, and when someone questioned my memory of something I insisted that I had remembered it correctly. But yesterday my husband reminded me that we were going to get the kids' Christmas presents at K-Mart last night, when I had thought we were going to wait until the weekend. I honestly can't remember which one we decided on, although I remember the discussion we had. I felt a flash of anger and started to argue, but then I realized, "Well, this is one of my symptoms. I guess I'll just go with the flow and not fuss about it." So I said, "Gosh, honey, I guess I remembered wrong. I thought we said we'd go this weekend. But let's do it tonight, anyway," and gave him a big smile. He was amazed and I felt relieved not to have to fight about who was right.

MY STANCE TOWARD LIFE IN CHILDHOOD WAS:

CHANGES I HAVE NOTED:

A REASSESSMENT

Since recovery in the previous two symptoms concerning experiencing self-esteem and having appropriate boundaries predictably affects recovery in this symptom of owning one's reality, you may now be on a different level concerning owning your reality.

WHAT TO DO

Reassess your level of awareness of your own reality at this time using the following chart. Place an X in the appropriate box for each area of reality.

My Reassessment of Owning My Reality

LEVEL OF AWARENESS	PHYSICAL REALITY	THINKING REALITY	FEELING REALITY	BEHAVIORAL REALITY
LEVEL A				
LEVEL B				
HEALTHY				

Level A: Know your reality but won't tell.

Level B: Don't know what your reality is.

Healthy: Know your reality and can own it when appropriate.

CHANGES IN OWNING SPECIFIC AREAS OF REALITY

Now we will deal with each area of reality individually. Spend some time on each area, following these guidelines:

1. In a quiet place, read the instructions for one area, then meditate for at least fifteen minutes (more if you wish) about your life as related to that particular area of reality. Write the insights that come to you during your meditation in the space provided. If no insights come, repeat your meditation about that area of reality for several days until insights come.

For each area where you have assessed yourself as being at level A, begin to own your reality by writing about an example of that type of reality you have not been willing to share with another safe person. Then share it with someone safe or at a Twelve-Step meeting, and write about how you felt as you acknowledged your reality to someone.

For each area where you have assessed yourself as being at level B, describe various aspects of that area of your reality to the best of your ability. When you consciously own *something*, even if you know it isn't exactly right, your subconscious mind will often gradually surrender knowledge from which you have been cut off, and you can begin to know what your reality is. Then go back and correct whatever you have previously written with the more accurate knowledge.

2. Attend a Twelve-Step meeting such as Codependents Anonymous and share your awareness of yourself in each area of reality. Listen for others to share on the same subject and try to let what you hear lead you to insights about yourself. If attending a meeting is not possible, call a fellow Twelve-Step member or your sponsor and briefly talk about your awareness of yourself. Ask that person what his or her experience has been with awareness of this area and listen for insights that apply to you. Write about any insights that come to you as a result of either of these experiences.

WHAT TO DO

Write about changes in owning your reality in each of the four areas.

YOUR PHYSICAL REALITY

Use the following space to record any changes you have made as a result of beginning to acknowledge your *physical appearance*.

Possibilities: Changes in the way you dress

Changes in your grooming procedures (shaving, hairstyle, makeup)

Recognizing that you are too heavy or too thin and taking steps to improve that

Greater acceptance of your physical characteristics (such as facial features, body size, certain bulges, height, weight)

Changes in Owning My Physical Appearance

Use the following space to record any changes you have made regarding your awareness of *how your body is functioning*.

Possibilities: Getting enough sleep

Getting a physical exam or dental checkup

Getting medical advice about a suspicious symptom

Doing reasonable exercise

Correcting constipation or chronic diarrhea

Taking care of headaches

Taking care of back pain

Changes in Owning My Body Functioning

THINKING REALITY

Use the following space to write about any changes you have made to own your thinking reality.

If you have been at level A, record incidents when you stated an opinion that you had previously been unable or unwilling to share; and record occasions when you were able to give your preference for a restaurant, movie, or other activity you shared with someone else. Whether you ended up doing what you preferred or not, did you share your preference?

If you have been at level B, write your best guess about what your thinking is on a subject that has come up for discussion in your presence recently; and write your answer to a frequently asked question in your life, such as "Where shall we go out to eat?" or "What do you want to do tonight?"

Changes in Owning My Thinking Reality

FEELING REALITY

Use the following space to write about any changes you have made in owning your own emotional reality.

If you have been at level A, record any incidents when you were able to express an emotion you had previously held in (for example, at a meeting, with your spouse or significant other, with a friend, with a therapist).

If you have been at level B, write your best guess about what your feelings are on an issue that has come up recently. Some examples of possible issues are (1) someone was late for an appointment with you; (2) someone close to you has been seriously ill; (3) you yourself have a serious illness. (After you have done this, your authentic emotions will often gradually surface later and you can correct this guess with the more accurate knowledge of your feeling reality.)

Changes in Owning My Feeling Reality

BEHAVIORAL REALITY

Use the following space to write about how you have begun to acknowledge your own behavior.

If you have been at level A, write about a behavior you have not been willing to acknowledge to another person before. Remember that behavior includes both shortcomings and accomplishments. Later, after you have told someone about your behavior or talked about it at a Twelve-Step meeting, write short sentences about the behavior you are now beginning to own.

EXAMPLE	I told my sponsor I am often late to aftercare.
	I told some of my friends I did a good job on the report I handed in at work.
	I told my wife I forgot to mail her letters until a day later.

If you have been at level B, write your best guess about what you have done or not done. Possibilities include what you might have done with an item you have lost, or the impact of your behavior on your spouse and children, your employees or co-workers, your friends.

Changes in Owning My Behavioral Reality

TRACKING IMPROVEMENT

Recovery in this symptom of owning your own reality leads to a general sense of being comfortable with yourself as a perfectly imperfect, fallible person.

WHAT TO DO

Record instances in which you have noticed your own imperfection and experienced less discomfort than before.

Signs of Improvement in Owning My Imperfection

Acknowledging and Meeting
Your Own Needs and Wants

Now that your are experiencing some recovery in the areas of self-esteem, boundaries, and owning your own reality, you can turn to acknowledging and meeting your own needs and wants. As a functional recovering adult, you are responsible for meeting your own needs and wants. You take care of those needs that you can meet on your own but you ask for help from appropriate sources with meeting the ones that no one can meet alone, such as the needs for emotional and physical nurture. You acknowledge both little wants and big wants and take steps to meet them for yourself or with the cooperation of others.

PURPOSE OF EXERCISES

These exercises are designed to help you (1) move out of whatever codependent condition you experience with needs and wants, toward interdependence; (2) identify and go about meeting your own needs; (3) identify your own wants, both big and little, and meet those that are feasible and appropriate.

BACKGROUND READING

(1) Review pages 28–34 of *Facing Codependence*, concerning the symptom of difficulty acknowledging and meeting needs and wants. (2) Review pages 85–88 of *Facing Codependence*, concerning a child's dependency in a dysfunctional family. (3) Review your writing in Step One in this workbook about how you experience this symptom.

Recovery from this symptom involves practicing awareness and taking the steps necessary to meet your needs and wants. The following exercises provide space to record your emerging awareness and successes in meeting needs and wants, taking responsibility for yourself when appropriate, and asking for help when appropriate.

A REASSESSMENT

Now that you have begun to experience recovery in the previous three symptoms, changes may have occurred in your level of awareness in this symptom since you made your original assessment in Step One.

WHAT TO DO

Reassess yourself now using the following charts. Mark an X in the appropriate box in each column of the charts.

My Reassessment of How I Meet Needs

Level of Functioning	Food	Clothing	Shelter	Physical Nurturing	Emotional Nurturing	Medical/ Dental Attention	Sexual Info. & Guidance	Financial Info. & Guidance
Too dependent								
Anti- dependent								
Needless/ wantless								
Confuse needs with wants								
Healthy								

Too dependent: I know I have needs but I don't acknowledge or take care of them.

Antidependent: I know I have needs but I do not or cannot ask for help.

Needless: I am unaware I have needs.

Confuse needs with wants: I take care of needs (of which I am unaware) by getting what I want (which I can recognize).

Healthy: I acknowledge and meet my needs.

My Reassessment of How I Meet Wants

LEVEL OF FUNCTIONING	LITTLE WANTS (PREFERENCES)	BIG WANTS (AFFECTING LIFE GOALS)
TOO DEPENDENT		
ANTIDEPENDENT		
WANTLESS		
CONFUSE WANTS WITH NEEDS		
HEALTHY		

Too dependent: I know what I want but expect others to meet my wants.

Antidependent: I know what I want but do not or cannot ask for help.

Wantless: I don't know what I want.

Confuse wants with needs: I get wants met in an attempt to meet needs.

Healthy: I acknowledge my wants and meet them.

CHANGES IN YOUR LEVEL OF FUNCTIONING

WHAT TO DO Use the following space to write about changes you have noticed in your level of functioning regarding wants and needs.

TOO DEPENDENT WITH NEEDS: I know what my needs are but expect others to meet them for me.

If you assessed yourself as too dependent with needs, in recovery you begin to meet the needs you can meet for yourself without relying on others. Write below the needs you have begun to provide for yourself.

Needs I Now Meet for Myself

ANTIDEPENDENT WITH NEEDS: I know I have needs but cannot or will not ask for help when another person is required to meet the need.

If you have been unable to ask for help in the past, in recovery you begin to risk asking safe people for help with the needs that require assistance. Use the space below to write about experiences you now have when you ask someone to help you meet a need.

Possibilities:

- when you need a hug or back rub (physical nurture)

- when you need to be sexual

- when you need directions to go somewhere

- when you need clarification of someone's instructions

- when you need financial advice

- when you need medical attention

- when you need to talk about a problem or share a feeling

Changes in Asking for Help with Needs

NEEDLESS: I am unaware that I have needs.

If you are needless trying to move to awareness of your needs, you will not automatically know what you need. All people have the basic needs I discussed earlier in this workbook, needs for food, clothing, shelter, physical nurture, emotional nurture, medical/dental attention, financial information, sex, and sexual information. After reviewing the questions about needs on pages 51–53 of this workbook, write in the space below needs you have become aware of that you were not aware of before.

Possibilities:

· the need for a hug or massage (physical nurture)

· the need for time, attention, and direction

· the need for medical or dental examinations

· the need for financial information

· the need for help preparing meals when you are sick

· the need for shelter when you have lost your job and cannot provide shelter for yourself or your family

Needs I Have Become Aware Of

When you move from being needless into being aware of your needs, you may move into antidependence regarding those needs: you now know what you need, but cannot or do not ask for help when another person is required to meet the need. If you are at this place (aware of needs but not getting the help you need), go back to the previous exercise and work on experiences you have as you begin to get assistance to meet these needs.

CONFUSING WANTS WITH NEEDS: I take care of needs (of which I am unaware) by getting what I want (which I can recognize).

If you have focused on your wants while neglecting some of your needs, or gotten things you want in an attempt to satisfy needs, in recovery you begin to identify the needs you were attempting to meet, and meet them directly. In the following space write down needs you have been trying to meet with wants that you are now meeting directly.

Possibilities:

- needing appropriate clothes for work, but spending clothing money on "fun" clothes that you want

- needing to develop friends for emotional nurture but buying a new car and spending your time in the car

- needing to share your feelings but eating an ice cream sundae instead

- needing help with your fears about not having enough money, but going on a spending spree getting whatever you want to reassure yourself about money

Needs I No Longer Meet with Wants, But Meet Directly

TOO DEPENDENT WITH WANTS: I know what my wants are but expect others to provide them for me.

If you assessed yourself as too dependent with wants, in recovery you begin to provide yourself with your wants. Write below the wants you have begun to provide for yourself.

Wants I Can Provide for Myself

ANTIDEPENDENT WITH WANTS: I know I have wants, but I cannot or will not ask for help with them.

If in the past you could not or did not ask for what you wanted when it required asking someone else for help, write in the following space about experiences you are now having when you do ask someone to help you.

Possibilities:

· when you want to go dancing or take ballroom dancing lessons

· when you want to invite guests to your home

· when you want to share a movie with someone

· when you want to ask a salesperson to help you try on clothes

Changes in Asking for Help with Wants

WANTLESS: I am unaware that I have wants.

If you are wantless trying to move to awareness of your wants, you will not automatically know what you want. To recover, you have to make guesses about what you think you want. In the normal growing-up process, a child learns about wants like this: the child thinks he or she wants something, makes the decision to get it, gets it, then finds out if he or she really wants it or not. So some of the things you think you want will turn out to be something you really don't want, and that is normal. It is the process of wanting something, getting it, and discovering whether or not you really want it that teaches you about your own wants.

To begin to recover from being wantless, try to prime the pump by guessing at a few things you think you might want. List them in the following chart. Next, attain this want for yourself and evaluate whether it brings you joy. Write "Yes" or "No" beside each item in the list that you get, according to whether or not you enjoyed it.

Things I Think I Might Want, But I'm Not Sure	*Brought Joy (Yes/No)*

Tracking Improvement

Recovery from this symptom means that you begin to experience interdependence. You are able to note your needs and wants and meet them for yourself. When you cannot meet them yourself, you are able to ask for help without shame or guilt. In recovery, as you move toward interdependence, you are also moving away from one or a combination of the four codependent stances:

Too dependent

Antidependent

Needless and wantless

Confusing wants with needs

What To Do

Use the following space to write about ways you are beginning to acknowledge and meet specific needs and wants. List the need or want, then describe what you are doing to meet it.

Ways I Am Beginning to Acknowledge and Meet Needs

Ways I Am Beginning to Acknowledge and Meet Wants

Experiencing and Expressing Your Reality Moderately

As a codependent, when you experience and express your physical, thinking, feeling, and behavioral reality, you are either immature and out of control or overmature and extremely controlling. This symptom is sometimes referred to as the either/or syndrome or the all-or-nothing approach to life. It is both a symptom in itself and a characteristic of each of the other four symptoms:

SYMPTOM	ONE EXTREME	THE OPPOSITE EXTREME
Self-esteem	less than	better than
Boundaries	too vulnerable	invulnerable
Owning reality	rebellious/bad	perfect/good
Meeting needs and wants	too dependent	antidependent or needless/wantless
Operating in extremes	immature/chaotic	overmature/controlling

PURPOSE OF EXERCISES

These exercises are designed (1) to guide you in reexamining your responses to specific situations so you can discover your extreme experiences or expressions, and (2) to provide a place to write about your experiences or expressions that are more moderate as you experience improvement.

BACKGROUND READING

(1) Review pages 35–42 of *Facing Codependence*, about the symptom of difficulty experiencing and expressing your reality moderately. (2) Review pages 88–89, about a child's immaturity in a dysfunctional family. (3) Review your writing in Step One about how you experience and express reality immoderately. (4) Read the following paragraphs.

As you have learned in *Facing Codependence*, this symptom begins with the way your caregivers responded to your childhood characteristics of immaturity. Depending on whether you were pushed to be more mature than your age or allowed to be less mature than your age, you developed a chaotic or a controlling approach to life. From either position, however, you experience reality immoderately.

By *chaotic,* I mean more than just lack of organization. It is an underfunctioning, spacy, haphazard, almost helpless approach to life that invites being rescued and controlled by others. And you are either grateful or rebellious toward those who try to rescue and control you. By *controlling,* I mean a rigid, manipulating, in-charge, inordinately responsible approach to life that you impose on yourself and others. You may often be angry and resentful or experience great pain when someone ignores, resists, or escapes your control.

In addition to these two characteristics, you have difficulty expressing your reality in a way that is appropriate for your age. You may present yourself physically as someone much younger or older than you actually are. Your thinking may be very young, naive, and immature, or you may put yourself through mental processes common for a much older person. Your anger may be of the two-year-old temper-tantrum variety or it may be expressed in the quiet, controlled voice of a saintly person wiser and more tolerant than you really are, while inside you are churning and fighting to control yourself. And your behavior may be childish or inordinately controlled and "old." In other words, if I and my daughter, who are both adults, are both in recovery and express our reality moderately, it will look, sound, and be different for her, a young woman in her twenties, than for me, a forty–six–year–old woman.

When you move toward recovery, you are able to be mature at your own age level (twenties, thirties, forties, fifties, sixties, seventies, and so on) more of the time. You can experience and express moderation in your appearance, thinking, feelings, and behavior.

Moderate responses usually feel very strange for a while to a codependent. In your own opinion (which is still coming out of codependence), you may think you aren't doing enough. Sometimes you may wonder whether people will think you don't care enough about their issues if you don't have extreme emotional reactions to them. But I believe as you continue to try to experience and express yourself with moderation, you will find a great improvement in your own sense of inner peace and in the atmosphere of your relationships.

WHAT TO DO

Use the following space to describe encounters in which you now realize your response was extreme. (Perhaps your thinking process created an extreme solution to a conflict, you were extremely emotional, or you did an extreme behavior.) After describing your extreme reaction, tell how you might have responded to the same situation with moderation.

EXAMPLE

THE SITUATION: My husband commented that I spent too much time fussing over picky details about meals.

MY EXTREME REACTION: Thinking—I decided, ''Okay, if that's his problem, I'll show him. I'll spend *no* time on meals. Then he'll know what he's missing.'' Feelings—I was hurt and felt unappreciated for all I do for him. Behavior—I served frozen dinners the rest of the week. I was sulky and distant and refused to talk to him about it further.

A MORE MODERATE RESPONSE: I could have talked to him about what he meant and why he was bringing it up. I might have learned that he just didn't think it was necessary to have four courses every night (soup, salad, entree, dessert) and homemade bread and other ''extras'' I've been serving. I might have learned that he wanted me to have more time with him in the evening and was willing to have less-elaborate meals to make that happen. I could have explored simpler recipes such as crock-pot dishes, casseroles from the freezer, and brown 'n' serve rolls. I could have saved my gourmet expertise for times when we entertain friends or special occasions like birthdays and anniversaries.

Situations to Which I've Made Extreme Responses

1. **THE SITUATION:**

   MY EXTREME REACTION:

   A MORE MODERATE RESPONSE:

2. **THE SITUATION:**

   MY EXTREME REACTION:

   A MORE MODERATE RESPONSE:

3. **THE SITUATION:**

   MY EXTREME REACTION:

   A MORE MODERATE RESPONSE:

Use the following space to write about incidents you are noticing in which you experience an area of reality with more moderation.

EXAMPLE

INCIDENT: My boss told me that he had noticed how often I was late returning to work after lunch during the past month and wanted me to be back on time.

REALITY AREA(S) INVOLVED: Thinking, feeling, behavior

MY RESPONSE AND HOW IT WAS MORE MODERATE: I was able to tolerate his noticing my imperfection. I did not launch into justifying my tardiness, I just realized that he was right. I felt guilt because I value being on time, and I felt shame because my imperfection was noticed, but it did not grow into the usual shame attack. I told my boss that I was sorry and I certainly would make it a point to be back on time. The next day I was back two minutes late instead of twenty minutes late, and I considered that a success. I didn't have to come back fifteen minutes early to PROVE I could be on time, like I used to do.

Incidents in Which I've Shown More Moderation

1. INCIDENT:

    REALITY AREA(S) INVOLVED:

    MY RESPONSE AND HOW IT WAS MORE MODERATE:

2. INCIDENT:

    REALITY AREA(S) INVOLVED:

    MY RESPONSE AND HOW IT WAS MORE MODERATE:

Whether you have acted younger or older than your age, experiencing your reality at your own age level is a mark of recovery. Use the following space to describe ways you are beginning to experience and express yourself closer to your own age level.

<table>
<tr><td>EXAMPLE</td><td>Physical reality: I am a sixty-five–year–old man. I played varsity basketball in college and have continued to seek out basketball games to keep in shape. For the last five years I've been playing at the health club with a bunch of guys in their twenties. I've suffered bruises and sprains and had to take time off to recuperate, but as soon as I could, back I'd go. I didn't want anyone to think I was a sissy. It's a wonder I didn't seriously hurt myself. Last week some guys in their sixties who go to my church invited me to play tennis with them one afternoon a week. I went and tried it and really liked being with physically fit men my own age. I can still keep in shape but compete with people who are at my level and have conversations about things I'm interested in at this stage of life.</td></tr>
</table>

Ways I'm Beginning to Act My Own Age

TRACKING IMPROVEMENT

Recovery from this symptom means experiencing moderation in your life in general.

WHAT TO DO

Use the following to describe ways you have noticed you are different—more moderate in your experience of the situation.

Possibilities: Telling a joke moderately

Cleaning house moderately

Planning a moderate vacation

Responding to a crisis moderately (with appropriate feelings, which may be strong but are not overwhelming and out of control)

Having a conversation, balancing listening with talking

Doing a moderate number of errands in one day

Giving moderate consequences to a child who has misbehaved

Handling a "no" response from someone moderately

Ways I Am Experiencing Life More Moderately

Recovering From Unmanageable Consequences

When you begin to experience improvement in the five core symptoms, their unmanageable consequences automatically begin to improve also. As you feel your own worth from inside more of the time, your need to exert negative control is not as strong. As you develop healthy boundaries, own your own reality, begin to meet your own needs and wants, and begin to experience and express yourself moderately, many of these secondary symptoms decrease in intensity.

PURPOSE OF EXERCISES

These exercises are designed to improve your awareness of how the unmanageable consequences heal themselves as you work on the five core symptoms. This section provides space for you to record incidents in which you notice recovery from these formerly unmanageable consequences.

BACKGROUND READING

Review chapter 3 of *Facing Codependence,* concerning unmanageable consequences stemming from the five symptoms of codependence. The unmanageable consequences are negative control, resentment, impaired spirituality, avoidance of reality, and inability to sustain intimacy.

WHAT TO DO

Each type of unmanageable consequence is dealt with individually in the following pages. Spend as much time as you need on each one. Read the instructions for one type of consequence, then spend some time reviewing your recent past in your mind. Look for the kinds of incidents called for, and write about any you remember. If you can't remember any, just spend time thinking about the consequence. Then put away the workbook and go about your day. During the day, try to be aware of times when you formerly would have experienced the consequence you are working on but do not anymore, or experience it less. Write about those examples in your workbook the next day. Continue this process focused on one consequence for several days before moving to the next one.

NEGATIVE CONTROL, PART 1

Use the following space to write about times you have noticed when you have exerted less effort to control any of the four parts of someone else's reality (the body, thinking, feelings, behavior) in situations in which you have exerted control in the past.

Times I've Exerted Less Negative Control

1. NAME:

Reality of the other person I used to try to control:

How I responded differently today from in the past:

2. NAME:

Reality of the other person I used to try to control:

How I responded differently today from in the past:

3. NAME:

Reality of the other person I used to try to control:

How I responded differently today from in the past:

NEGATIVE CONTROL, PART 2

Use the following space to write about times you have noticed when you have not allowed someone else to exert negative control over any of the four parts of your reality (your body, your thinking, your feelings, your behavior) in situations in which you have allowed your reality to be controlled in the past.

Times I Have Not Allowed Negative Control of Myself

1. NAME:

    Area of reality this person attempted to control:

    How I responded differently today from in the past:

2. NAME:

    Area of reality this person attempted to control:

    How I responded differently today from in the past:

3. NAME:

    Area of reality this person attempted to control:

    How I responded differently today from in the past:

RESENTMENT

Use the following space to write about experiences you have had in which you have noticed less resentment than you would have experienced before. Name the person involved and describe what happend and what used to happen (or would have happened, in your opinion).

Times I've Experienced Less Resentment

1. **NAME:**

   WHAT HAPPENED:

   WHAT USED TO HAPPEN:

2. **NAME:**

   WHAT HAPPENED:

   WHAT USED TO HAPPEN:

3. **NAME:**

   WHAT HAPPENED:

   WHAT USED TO HAPPEN:

SPIRITUALITY

Whether you have come from the position of denying all imperfection or that of thinking you are abnormally imperfect, at times in recovery you will be able to embrace some aspect of imperfection without an acute shame attack.

Use the following space to write about instances in which you have seen your own imperfection and have been able to accept it in yourself.

Times I've Embraced My Imperfection

1. **DATE:**

   IMPERFECTION:

2. **DATE:**

   IMPERFECTION:

3. **DATE:**

   IMPERFECTION:

In recovery, we are able to talk about our imperfection to others as well as to our Higher Power. Use the following space to write about times you have been able to do so. Name the person (or group) you have shared your imperfection with. Describe what you have said or done.

Times I've Shared My Imperfection

1. NAME OR GROUP: **DATE:**

    IMPERFECTION I SHARED AND HOW:

2. NAME OR GROUP: **DATE:**

    IMPERFECTION I SHARED AND HOW:

3. NAME OR GROUP: **DATE:**

    IMPERFECTION I SHARED AND HOW:

In recovery, we are able to see and hear someone else's imperfection without judging the person or having to change or fix him or her. Use the following space to write about times you have been able to do so. Name the person who shared his or her imperfection with you. Describe what you heard or saw and how you responded.

Times I've Listened to Someone Share His or Her Imperfection without Judgment or Attempting to Change the Person

1. **NAME:**

   Imperfection I listened to:

   How I responded differently today from in the past:

2. **NAME:**

   Imperfection I listened to:

   How I responded differently today from in the past:

3. **NAME:**

   Imperfection I listened to:

   How I responded differently today from in the past:

Describe in the following space your thoughts about the nature of the Higher Power and your relationship with the Higher Power. How are these changing as you experience recovery in this area of accepting your imperfection and relating to a Higher Power? When and how do you talk to your Higher Power?

My Thoughts About the Higher Power and Me

My thoughts about the nature of the Higher Power:

My relationship with the Higher Power:

How are the above changing as I experience recovery in accepting and sharing my imperfections?

When and how I talk to my Higher Power:

AVOIDANCE OF REALITY
(ADDICTIONS, PHYSICAL ILLNESS, MENTAL ILLNESS)

In recovery, we move closer and closer to the reality of our own personal experience, not necessarily "the Truth," but what is real for each of us—what we think, feel, do or not do, and how we look. As we get closer to this congruence, our reality becomes more in tune with the objective events in our lives than it was before. As we are able to face and deal with the reality of our lives and situations in which we find ourselves, we no longer need to cover and hide our feelings from ourselves with compulsions and addictive substances, physical illnesses, and mental disorders.

WHAT TO DO

Use the following space to write about experiences you have had recently that you have not medicated with an addiction (experiences that before recovery would have led to your medicating yourself). Name the former addiction, describe the situation, and describe what you did instead.

Experiences I Have Faced without Medication

---

1. ADDICTION: DATE:

    THE SITUATION:

    WHAT I DID INSTEAD:

---

2. ADDICTION: DATE:

    THE SITUATION:

    WHAT I DID INSTEAD:

Use the following space to note any chronic physical symptoms you have had that are improving (such as asthma, allergies, arthritis, hypertension, migraine headaches, psychosomatic pain of any kind). Name the symptom and describe how it has improved (for example, you need less medicine, it's been longer than ever since you had a headache or stomach ache).

Improvement in My Physical Symptoms

1. **PHYSICAL SYMPTOM:**   **DATE:**

    HOW IT IS BETTER:

2. **PHYSICAL SYMPTOM:**   **DATE:**

    HOW IT IS BETTER:

3. **PHYSICAL SYMPTOM:**   **DATE:**

    HOW IT IS BETTER:

Use the following space to write about situations that used to put you out of touch with reality (for example, profound depression, nervous breakdown) but that you have been able to deal with while staying in touch with reality. Describe the mental or emotional process you used to experience and how it is better.

Improvement in My Mental and Emotional Processes

1. DATE:

   MENTAL OR EMOTIONAL PROCESS:

   HOW IT IS BETTER:

2. DATE:

   MENTAL OR EMOTIONAL PROCESS:

   HOW IT IS BETTER:

INTIMACY

Intimacy involves both giving and receiving without judgment or attempts to change the other's reality or "fix" him or her. Use the following space to write about experiences of intimacy in which you have been able to *give* to the other person. Name the person, describe the area or areas of reality that you have shared (physical, thinking, feelings, behavior), and describe how you have shared.

Experiences of Giving Intimacy

1. NAME: **DATE:**

    AREAS OF REALITY:

    HOW I SHARED:

2. NAME: **DATE:**

    AREAS OF REALITY:

    HOW I SHARED:

3. NAME: **DATE:**

    AREAS OF REALITY:

    HOW I SHARED:

Use the following space to write about experiences of intimacy in which you have *received* from someone else. Perhaps your child told you some things he or she was thinking and you didn't interrupt to try to adjust his or her reality. Perhaps you felt a new physical closeness with your spouse or significant other. Name the person and describe what happened.

Experiences of Receiving Intimacy

1. **NAME:**   **DATE:**

   WHAT HAPPENED:

2. **NAME:**   **DATE:**

   WHAT HAPPENED:

3. **NAME:**   **DATE:**

   WHAT HAPPENED:

4. **NAME:**   **DATE:**

   WHAT HAPPENED:

A Final Note

This is not the end of recovery or even of breaking free from codependence. We are only beginning. But we are discovering that what began as a frantic attempt to find relief from pain, powerlessness, and unmanageable consequences in our relationships has become a way to see how all of life can fit together for us. We are beginning to enjoy living and the gifts and challenges we have been given with a sense of serenity and gratitude.

We have found that working the Twelve Steps, attending meetings regularly, reading, working with a sponsor (and being sponsors), and perhaps most of all beginning to trust our Higher Power with our wills and the recovery of our lives has led us to realize that life really can be different. In giving away what we are learning and receiving, we are finding the promises of the Twelve-Step program coming true in our lives, one day at a time.

Our wish for you and for us is that we will all continue to grow as we learn to live in healthy ways and to love ourselves, the other people in our lives, and our Higher Power—whom we choose to call God.

Pia Mellody
Andrea Wells Miller